ESSENTIAL SKILLS IN MATHS

BOOK 1

Nelson

Graham Newman and Ron Bull

First published in 1996 by:
Thomas Nelson and Sons Ltd

Reprinted in 2002 by:
Nelson Thornes Ltd
Delta Place
27 Bath Road
CHELTENHAM
GL53 7TH
United Kingdom

03 04 05 / 10 9

A catalogue record for this book is available from the British Library

ISBN 0-17-431440-X

Printed and bound in China

Contents

NUMBER

ALGEBRA

SHAPE, SPACE AND MEASURES

HANDLING DATA

Number

1/ WORDS TO NUMBERS

EXAMPLES

▶ Three hundred and twenty-seven = 327

Six million, five hundred thousand and thirty-five = 6 500 035

Exercise 1A

Write in number form.

1 Two hundred and twenty-six 226
2 Four hundred and eleven
3 Eight hundred and thirty-one 831
4 Three hundred and six
5 Five hundred and seventeen 517
6 Two hundred and thirteen
7 Six hundred and forty-four 644
8 Four thousand, two hundred and eighty-three
9 Seven thousand, three hundred and seventy-six 7376
10 Five thousand, nine hundred and sixty-seven
11 One thousand, nine hundred and fifteen 1915
12 Five thousand and six
13 Nine thousand, one hundred and nineteen 9119
14 Two hundred and fifty thousand
15 Seventy thousand, six hundred and twenty
16 Fifteen thousand, seven hundred and five
17 Seven thousand, six hundred and ten
18 Seventy-five thousand, six hundred
19 One million
20 One hundred thousand, five hundred and fifty

Exercise 1B

Write in number form.

1 Six hundred and forty-seven
2 Eight hundred and thirty-five
3 Nine hundred and fifty-four
4 One hundred and ten
5 Four hundred and eighty-eight
6 Three hundred and forty-six
7 Six hundred and twelve
8 Five thousand, six hundred and fourteen
9 Eleven thousand, seven hundred and twelve
10 Eighty thousand, six hundred
11 Seventeen thousand and seventy-six
12 Seventy-four thousand, five hundred
13 Twenty thousand, six hundred and fifty
14 Twenty-one thousand
15 Five thousand, four hundred and twenty-seven
16 Ten thousand, six hundred
17 Eighteen thousand, nine hundred and fifty-seven
18 One hundred and eight thousand, five hundred
19 Two million, five hundred thousand
20 Two hundred thousand, five hundred

Exercise 1C

Write in number form.

1. Five thousand, six hundred and thirty-nine
2. Six thousand, three hundred and twenty
3. Two thousand, seven hundred and forty-five
4. Six thousand and eight
5. Three thousand, one hundred and nine
6. Fifteen thousand, six hundred
7. Eleven thousand, three hundred
8. Eighteen thousand, seven hundred
9. Twenty-one thousand, eight hundred and fifty
10. Two hundred and fifty thousand, nine hundred
11. Seventy-five thousand, eight hundred and thirty
12. Three hundred and fifty thousand, two hundred
13. Fifty-five thousand, five hundred and forty
14. Three and a half million
15. Two hundred thousand and fifty
16. Seventy-five thousand and thirty
17. One million, five hundred thousand
18. Seven hundred and forty thousand
19. Eighty-eight thousand, nine hundred and fifty
20. Two million, five hundred thousand, six hundred

Exercise 1D

Write in number form.

1. Six thousand, seven hundred and eleven
2. Eight thousand, two hundred and twenty
3. Six thousand and fifty
4. Seven thousand, three hundred and twenty
5. Seventeen hundred and fifty
6. Nine thousand, seven hundred and twelve
7. Twelve thousand, five hundred
8. Twenty-five thousand
9. Fifteen thousand, seven hundred and forty
10. Sixty-seven thousand, eight hundred and thirty-eight
11. Forty-seven thousand, six hundred
12. Two hundred and five thousand, seven hundred
13. Seventy-five thousand, nine hundred and fifty
14. Thirty-nine thousand, one hundred
15. Five hundred thousand
16. One million, five hundred thousand
17. Four and a half million
18. One million, six hundred and fifty thousand
19. Twenty-five million
20. Four hundred and five thousand, five hundred

2/ NUMBERS TO WORDS

> **EXAMPLES**
> ▶ 12 500 = twelve thousand, five hundred
>
> 5 050 675 = five million, fifty thousand, six hundred and seventy-five

Exercise 2A

Write these numbers in words.

1 750	**2** 465	**3** 205	**4** 467	**5** 981
6 690	**7** 1450	**8** 3850	**9** 2754	**10** 9800
11 18 505	**12** 17 015	**13** 12 013	**14** 165 450	**15** 105 875
16 100 050	**17** 1 000 000	**18** 170 010	**19** 850 750	**20** 5 506 820

Exercise 2B

Write these numbers in words.

1 365	**2** 506	**3** 212	**4** 523	**5** 915
6 750	**7** 898	**8** 3550	**9** 5670	**10** 4050
11 27 750	**12** 36 450	**13** 75 430	**14** 305 000	**15** 225 570
16 2 000 000	**17** 3 500 000	**18** 45 000 000	**19** 20 012	**20** 2 780 050

Exercise 2C

Write these numbers in words.

1 2500	**2** 2650	**3** 4568	**4** 7708	**5** 1018
6 3905	**7** 6541	**8** 25 000	**9** 75 700	**10** 19 470
11 100 000	**12** 125 000	**13** 25 050	**14** 167 900	**15** 225 609
16 12 000 000	**17** 75 000	**18** 340 150	**19** 110 011	**20** 107 895

Exercise 2D

Write these numbers in words.

1 3500	**2** 3450	**3** 4804	**4** 2001	**5** 5070
6 1112	**7** 8907	**8** 25 000	**9** 34 500	**10** 75 600
11 37 045	**12** 185 000	**13** 650 000	**14** 100 040	**15** 25 768
16 3 000 000	**17** 4 500 000	**18** 347 890	**19** 200 680	**20** 1 700 500

3/ THE VALUE OF A GIVEN DIGIT WITHIN A NUMBER

The value of a digit within a number depends upon its position in that number.

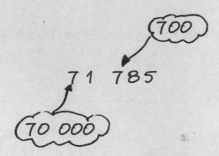

There are two 7s in **71 7**85 but the first one has a value of 70 000 (seventy thousand) and the second has a value of 700 (seven hundred).

EXAMPLE

▶ State the value of each underlined digit in number form: 2̲54 58̲7.

   The 2 has the value 200 000.   The 7 has the value 7 units.

EXAMPLE

▶ State the value of each underlined digit in word form: 3̲ 3̲25 681.

   The 3 has the value three million.   The 2 has the value twenty thousand.

EXAMPLE

▶ State the value of each underlined digit in number form: 3̲5̲ 082.

   The 3 has the value 30 000.   The 5 has the value 5 000.

Exercise 3A

Write the value of each underlined digit in **number form.**

1	6̲53 *600*	**2**	8̲47	**3**	3̲42	**4**	10̲44	**5**	7̲562
6	9̲143 *9100*	**7**	85̲9̲9	**8**	37̲46	**9**	8̲231	**10**	25̲607
11	32̲554 *32500*	**12**	15̲925	**13**	29̲684	**14**	97̲548	**15**	57̲563

Write the value of each underlined digit in **word form.**

16	3̲25	**17**	6̲53	**18**	7̲29	**19**	2̲652	**20**	7̲825
21	8̲027	**22**	6̲176	**23**	97̲58	**24**	3̲412	**25**	8̲745
26	31̲45̲7	**27**	15̲721	**28**	21̲964	**29**	58̲17̲5	**30**	37̲619

Exercise 3B

Write the value of each underlined digit in **number form**.

1	5<u>4</u>2	**2**	4<u>3</u>6	**3**	<u>3</u>72	**4**	21<u>7</u>4	**5**	25<u>4</u>7
6	317<u>5</u>	**7**	9<u>3</u>78	**8**	261<u>7</u>	**9**	33<u>5</u>4	**10**	<u>2</u>6 273
11	<u>31</u> 065	**12**	25 <u>6</u>34	**13**	64 9<u>1</u>2	**14**	<u>32</u> 543	**15**	12<u>9</u>7<u>5</u>

Write the value of each underlined digit in **word form**.

16	<u>5</u>21	**17**	<u>5</u>64	**18**	<u>7</u>13	**19**	2<u>7</u>34	**20**	61<u>3</u>6
21	74<u>05</u>	**22**	300<u>7</u>	**23**	6<u>3</u>52	**24**	1<u>9</u>25	**25**	83 <u>6</u>09
26	<u>32</u> 017	**27**	45 <u>1</u>06	**28**	<u>7</u>0 3<u>8</u>5	**29**	64 <u>3</u>38	**30**	<u>8</u>1 206

Exercise 3C

Write the value of each underlined digit in **number form**.

1	33<u>6</u>4	**2**	24<u>78</u>	**3**	<u>5</u>126	**4**	23 <u>7</u>54	**5**	18 59<u>7</u>
6	3<u>29</u>5	**7**	89 <u>3</u>15	**8**	190 <u>2</u>83	**9**	<u>2</u>72 104	**10**	1 12<u>5</u> 756
11	3 <u>4</u>17 <u>6</u>59	**12**	<u>7</u>8 451 950	**13**	<u>5</u>10 28<u>7</u>	**14**	3 0<u>67</u> 249	**15**	1<u>37</u> 928

Write the value of each underlined digit in **word form**.

16	21<u>6</u>9	**17**	413<u>5</u>	**18**	6<u>7</u>51	**19**	12<u>9</u>64	**20**	64 17<u>5</u>
21	11<u>4</u> 7<u>1</u>2	**22**	72 3<u>84</u>	**23**	<u>2</u>56 035	**24**	<u>5</u>4 628	**25**	8 <u>1</u>00 670
26	2 <u>3</u>40 <u>8</u>60	**27**	<u>2</u>1 006 351	**28**	7 58<u>9</u> 056	**29**	<u>61</u>5 633	**30**	1 1<u>2</u>9 817

Exercise 3D

Write the value of each underlined digit in **number form**.

1	<u>5</u>732	**2**	22<u>8</u>4	**3**	6<u>1</u>72	**4**	18 <u>3</u>56	**5**	<u>25</u> 765
6	76 6<u>5</u>3	**7**	235 <u>4</u>63	**8**	135 <u>7</u>54	**9**	<u>3</u>9 231	**10**	810 <u>6</u>17
11	<u>1</u> 256 654	**12**	2 <u>8</u>57 <u>9</u>25	**13**	25 2<u>5</u>0 998	**14**	<u>1</u> 121 <u>2</u>54	**15**	13 7<u>5</u>0 695

Write the value of each underlined digit in **word form**.

16	3<u>654</u>	**17**	<u>1</u>075	**18**	4<u>2</u>19	**19**	12 <u>5</u>45	**20**	32 <u>7</u>43
21	25 <u>9</u>84	**22**	<u>2</u>83 115	**23**	3<u>3</u>5 007	**24**	<u>7</u>2 738	**25**	2 <u>0</u>07 650
26	32 5<u>4</u>0 060	**27**	<u>4</u> 750 000	**28**	<u>9</u>7 400 000	**29**	21 11<u>7</u> 533	**30**	5 <u>6</u>70 050

4/ ORDERING NUMBERS

When placing numbers in order of size, this can be in *ascending* or *descending* order.

Ascending order is when the numbers start with the *smallest* number and *increase* in size to reach the largest number at the end.

Descending order is the reverse: starting *large* and getting *smaller*.

> **EXAMPLE**
>
> ▶ Write the numbers in descending order: 678, 197, 575, 975, 876
>
>   975, 876, 678, 575, 197

> **EXAMPLE**
>
> ▶ Write the numbers in ascending order: 1895, 2534, 987, 735, 6776, 509
>
>   509, 735, 987, 1895, 2534, 6776

Exercise 4A

Write the numbers in the order stated.

1   45, 78, 54, 106   (ascending)
2   91, 46, 87, 127   (ascending)
3   34, 79, 63, 31   (descending)
4   147, 193, 89, 235   (descending)
5   92, 86, 143, 742   (ascending)
6   861, 531, 854, 165   (ascending)
7   201, 87, 365, 109   (descending)
8   468, 487, 462, 395   (descending)
9   301, 813, 531, 943   (ascending)
10 813, 633, 512, 811, 755   (ascending)
11 381, 173, 286, 298, 98   (descending)
12 356, 384, 361, 321, 354   (descending)
13 4561, 4210, 4820, 4653   (descending)
14 4231, 4123, 4230, 4112   (ascending)
15 3541, 3521, 3519, 3531   (ascending)
16 2698, 2568, 754, 2684, 2465   (descending)
17 8621, 8736, 8465, 9100, 7564   (descending)
18 5866, 5799, 5864, 6012, 5763   (descending)
19 7986, 8975, 8644, 997, 7556   (ascending)
20 4862, 5367, 6233, 7784, 8886   (descending)

Exercise 4B

Write the numbers in the order stated.

1   55, 64, 26, 86   (ascending)
2   86, 68, 78, 64   (ascending)
3   32, 23, 31, 19   (ascending)
4   145, 165, 232, 172   (ascending)
5   269, 267, 176, 354   (descending)
6   802, 799, 789, 832   (descending)
7   730, 699, 823, 864   (ascending)
8   400, 398, 401, 389   (ascending)
9   258, 254, 245, 265   (descending)
10 806, 832, 866, 789, 846   (descending)

11	590, 500, 531, 578, 574 (ascending)	**12**	868, 986, 798, 879, 795 (ascending)
13	1024, 1032, 1231, 1203 (descending)	**14**	4006, 4566, 4060, 4022 (ascending)
15	5987, 986, 6488, 5897 (ascending)		
16	4683, 3967, 4610, 5564, 3977 (descending)		
17	8779, 8977, 8577, 978, 8634 (descending)		
18	7982, 745, 8001, 9002, 7888 (descending)		
19	2487, 2665, 3112, 3110, 2556 (ascending)		
20	5666, 6665, 6655, 5566, 5556 (ascending)		

Exercise 4C

Write the numbers in the order stated.

1	3120, 3211, 3224, 3222 (ascending)	**2**	2645, 3587, 1997, 2640 (ascending)
3	6898, 6897, 6543, 8856 (ascending)	**4**	2642, 2645, 685, 6851 (ascending)
5	7663, 7661, 7884, 7225 (ascending)	**6**	3986, 6733, 5001, 6862 (descending)
7	3894, 6932, 6732, 6532 (descending)	**8**	5656, 6565, 6656, 6555 (descending)
9	6846, 10 223, 14 561, 5986 (descending)		

10 15 687, 105 551, 114 364, 99 866 (ascending)

11 8654, 801 633, 88 330, 800 221 (descending)

12 687 800, 688 722, 668 566, 678 600 (ascending)

13 3 000 001, 3 000 210, 3 000 009, 3 000 007 (descending)

14 1 250 000, 1 750 000, 998 000, 500 000 (ascending)

15 99 000, 100 000, 98 500, 101 500 (ascending)

16 5 000 000, 487 000, 4 999 999, 885 000 (ascending)

17 6 000 500, 5 980 000, 6 100 000, 5 875 000 (descending)

18 4 005 000, 4 050 000, 405 999, 498 999 (descending)

19 3 500 000, 3 650 500, 2 900 000, 4 000 000 (descending)

20 1 001 500, 1 100 000, 1 000 000, 1 005 500 (descending)

Exercise 4D

Write the numbers in the order stated.

1	999, 1025, 1320, 1254 (descending)	**2**	5011, 5100, 4900, 4908 (descending)
3	2003, 1890, 1752, 2100 (descending)	**4**	3666, 3265, 3865, 4654 (descending)
5	8669, 8763, 7986, 7622 (descending)	**6**	8702, 8955, 8642, 887 (ascending)
7	6284, 6332, 6223, 6731 (ascending)	**8**	4110, 4211, 5230, 5102 (ascending)
9	38 560, 37 500, 38 600, 7850 (ascending)		

10 2 000 400, 200 500, 2 001 000, 999 000 (descending)

11 1 500 000, 1 800 000, 1 550 000, 1 080 000 (ascending)

12 1 000 900, 1 100 000, 1 400 500, 1 000 500 (descending)

13 98 800, 78 540, 100 000, 99 500 (ascending)

14 2 000 500, 2 050 000, 999 000, 199 500   (descending)

15 998 600, 999 000, 99 999, 988 800   (descending)

16 2 240 000, 2 450 000, 245 000, 2 450 500   (descending)

17 465 200, 49 900, 456 000, 965 000   (ascending)

18 2 000 000, 2 500 000, 250 000, 2 650 500   (ascending)

19 65 550, 541 200, 158 650, 223 000, 684 100   (ascending)

20 123 500, 12 350, 238 400, 850 000, 98 600   (ascending)

5/ CONVERTING POUNDS TO PENCE AND PENCE TO POUNDS

There are 100 pence in £1. This means that multiplying by 100 changes pounds into pence.

> **EXAMPLE**
> ▶ £5 = 5 × 100p
>
>   = 500p

> **EXAMPLE**
> ▶ £2.16 = 2.16 × 100p
>
>   = 216p (move the decimal point two places to the right)

Converting pence to pounds requires division by 100.

> **EXAMPLE**
> ▶ 76p = £76 ÷ 100
>
>   = £0.76

> **EXAMPLE**
> ▶ 256p = £256 ÷ 100
>
>   = £2.56 (move the decimal point two places to the left)

Exercise 5A

Convert to pence.

1 £4 *400p*	**2** £2 *200p*	**3** £8 *800p*	**4** £6 *600p*	**5** £11 *1100p*
6 £3.54 *354p*	**7** £5.71 *571p*	**8** £3.75 *375p*	**9** £4.75 *475p*	**10** £7.50 *750p*
11 £8.96 *896p*	**12** £12.16 *1216p*	**13** £17.35 *1735p*	**14** £15.25 *1525p*	**15** £25.60 *2560p*
16 £14.38 *1438p*	**17** £16.80 *1680p*	**18** £28.68 *2868p*	**19** £30.62 *3062p*	**20** £20.05 *2005p*

Exercise 5B

Convert to pence.

1 £5	**2** £9	**3** £7	**4** £6.40	**5** £6.60
6 £17.85	**7** £13.06	**8** £11.55	**9** £39.78	**10** £21.31
11 £30.46	**12** £45.87	**13** £63.84	**14** £100.30	**15** £120.40
16 £251.63	**17** £187.06	**18** £350.75	**19** £466.44	**20** £204.32

Exercise 5C

Convert to pounds.

1	57p	**2**	65p	**3**	89p	**4**	62p	**5**	125p
6	650p	**7**	175p	**8**	204p	**9**	295p	**10**	1200p
11	1460p	**12**	1750p	**13**	1054p	**14**	890p	**15**	3875p
16	1453p	**17**	2835p	**18**	1108p	**19**	1945p	**20**	4006p

Exercise 5D

Convert to pounds.

1	84p	**2**	65p	**3**	89p	**4**	126p	**5**	187p
6	206p	**7**	156p	**8**	1425p	**9**	2896p	**10**	1170p
11	1063p	**12**	3280p	**13**	1445p	**14**	26 523p	**15**	12 323p
16	20 514p	**17**	31 225p	**18**	47 880p	**19**	35 400p	**20**	62 405p

6/ ADDITION AND SUBTRACTION OF MONEY

Exercise 6A

1	£1.34 + £1.65 £1.99	**2**	£4.63 + £2.24	**3**	£5.75 − £1.24	**4**	£4.65 − £2.45
5	£3.64 − £1.43 ±4	**6**	£6.74 + £1.25	**7**	£3.84 + £2.57	**8**	£2.15 + £6.05
9	£3.96 − £1.68	**10**	£2.57 − £1.58	**11**	£1.89 + £2.54	**12**	£4.54 − £2.62
13	£3.66 − £1.57	**14**	£7.35 + £2.65	**15**	£7.01 − £5.85	**16**	£6.95 + £2.88
17	£2.30 + £6.57	**18**	£7.10 − £4.25	**19**	£3.86 − £1.58	**20**	£6.85 + £1.63
21	£9.26 − £8.75	**22**	£1.56 + £5.84	**23**	£4.50 − £3.41	**24**	£5.00 − £3.85
25	£2.68 + £5.39	**26**	£8.05 − £4.06	**27**	£5.14 + £2.47	**28**	£4.76 + £1.98
29	£3.09 + £5.49	**30**	£4.22 − £1.74				

Exercise 6B

1	£2.50 + £3.64	**2**	£3.43 + £2.48	**3**	£6.29 − £4.36	**4**	£3.21 + £4.69
5	£5.40 − £2.68	**6**	£6.36 − £1.78	**7**	£5.86 + £2.25	**8**	£4.59 − £1.30
9	£7.82 − £4.65	**10**	£2.09 + £6.66	**11**	£1.67 + £3.08	**12**	£8.75 − £6.71
13	£9.00 − £5.55	**14**	£2.58 + £6.69	**15**	£8.06 − £3.28	**16**	£7.95 − £4.48
17	£4.89 + £2.27	**18**	£3.31 + £6.67	**19**	£2.84 + £7.16	**20**	£6.08 − £2.98
21	£4.60 − £2.08	**22**	£4.15 + £4.77	**23**	£8.25 − £3.39	**24**	£3.06 + £2.24
25	£2.95 + £7.75	**26**	£7.29 − £5.54	**27**	£5.11 − £3.22	**28**	£4.06 + £2.95
29	£6.00 − £5.83	**30**	£7.01 + £2.89				

7/ TOTALLING SUMS OF MONEY

EXAMPLE

▶ Add up these sums of money: three £10, seven £5, eight £1, four 50p, six 20p and eight 2p.

Pounds: £30 + £35 + £8 = £73
Pence: 200p + 120p + 16p = 336p = £3.36
Total: £73 + £3.36 = £76.36

Exercise 7A

Add up these sums of money.

1   Five 10p, eight 5p and ten 2p   £1.10
2   Four 50p, seven 20p and eight 5p
3   Two 20p, three 10p and five 5p
4   Three £1, three 50p, six 10p and eight 1p
5   Five 50p, four 20p, six 10p and five 2p
6   Nine 10p, ten 5p, eleven 2p and seven 1p
7   Five 20p, seven 10p, two 5p and seven 2p
8   Five £1, one 50p, four 20p and one 10p
9   Three £1, three 50p, seven 10p and two 5p
10 Six £1, two 50p, one 20p and eleven 10p
11 One £5, eighteen £1, six 50p and eight 10p
12 Two £10, three £5, seven £1 and two 50p
13 Seven £5, one £1, three 50p and eight 10p
14 Seven £5, eleven £1, nine 50p and eight 20p
15 Five £5, two £1, six 20p and eight 10p
16 One £20, five £10, six £5 and nine £1

Exercise 7B

Add up these sums of money.

1   Three 50p, five 20p and seven 5p
2   Six 20p, five 10p and eight 2p
3   Five 50p, ten 20p and four 5p
4   Six 20p, eight 10p, seven 5p and twenty 2p
5   Two 50p, three 10p, nine 5p and twelve 1p
6   Five 20p, eight 10p, six 5p and eight 2p
7   Three 50p, six 20p, ten 10p and twenty-five 1p
8   Nine £1, eight 50p, six 10p and seven 2p
9   Seven £1, three 50p, eight 20p and ten 10p
10 Two £5, four £1, seven 50p and ten 20p

11   One £10, six £5, eight £1 and seven 50p

12   Five £20, four £10, seven £5, four £1, eight 50p

13   Two £20, four £5, twelve £1 and eight 20p

14   Eight £5, seven £1, eight 20p and nine 10p

15   Six £1, eleven 50p, seven 20p and six 5p

16   Two £10, five £5, four £1, seven 50p and seven 20p

Exercise 7C

Add up these sums of money.

1   Six £1, one 50p, two 20p and one 5p

2   Eight £1, ten 20p and seven 5p

3   Thirty 20p, twenty-five 10p and eight 2p

4   Four £1, seven 50p, four 20p and seven 10p

5   Three £1, nine 50p, three 20p, ten 10p and nine 1p

6   Sixty-five 20p, forty-two 10p and thirty-four 2p

7   Eleven £1, eight 50p, three 20p, six 10p, eight 5p and five 1p

8   Three £5, four £1, one 50p and seven 20p

9   Two £10, five £5, ten £1 and six 50p

10   Five £1, eleven 50p, nine 20p, seven 10p, nine 5p and twenty 1p

11   Six £5, four £1, six 50p, nine 20p, twelve 2p

12   Two £20, five £10, eight £5, ten £1 and forty 50p

13   One £20, eight £5, seven £1, one 50p, ten 20p

14   Six £10, four £5, three £1, one 50p, five 20p, two 10p and fourteen 1p

15   One £20, seven £10, nine £5 and twenty-two £1

16   One £20, six £10, ten £5, sixteen £1, five 50p and ten 20p

Exercise 7D

Add up these sums of money.

1   Three £1, two 50p, six 10p and five 5p

2   Nine £1, seven 50p, seven 20p and six 10p

3   Eighteen 50p, twenty-one 20p, nineteen 10p and seven 2p

4   Six £1, eight 20p, seven 10p, five 2p and eleven 1p

5   Nine 50p, twelve 20p, eight 10p and six 5p

6   One £1, fourteen 50p, seven 20p and eighteen 10p

7   Thirty-two 20p, twenty-eight 10p, seventeen 5p and twelve 2p

8   Five £5, sixteen £1, seven 50p and nineteen 10p

9   Three £10, six £5, fifteen £1 and seven 50p

10   Eight £5, fourteen £1, twenty-two 50p, sixteen 20p and nineteen 10p

11   Seventeen £1, fourteen 50p, seven 20p, six 10p and nine 5p

12   Seven 50p, nine 20p, seven 10p, nine 5p and five 2p

13   Four £20, three £10, nine £5, fifteen £1 and nine 50p

14   Seven £5, twelve £1, fourteen 50p, ten 20p and nine 10p

15   Twelve £5, eighteen £1, seventeen 50p, six 20p and eighteen 10p

16   Eleven £1, eight 50p, eight 20p, nine 10p, seven 5p and twenty-four 2p

8/ MENTAL ARITHMETIC: ADDING AND SUBTRACTING

These questions are for **mental** arithmetic. Try to do all the calculations in your head without writing down any working. Do *not* use a calculator.

Exercise 8A

1	7 + 8 15	**2**	6 + 4	**3**	8 + 12	**4**	3 + 7	**5**	7 + 6
6	18 – 7 5	**7**	13 – 9	**8**	12 – 4	**9**	16 – 7	**10**	20 – 11
11	9 + 5 14	**12**	8 + 9	**13**	14 – 6	**14**	16 – 4	**15**	4 + 16
16	5 + 13 18	**17**	14 – 5	**18**	18 – 9	**19**	6 + 4	**20**	7 + 5
21	11 – 8 3	**22**	16 – 8	**23**	17 – 9	**24**	20 – 5	**25**	6 + 12
26	15 + 5 20	**27**	11 + 8	**28**	19 – 12	**29**	17 – 14	**30**	12 + 6
31	9 + 12 21	**32**	8 + 14	**33**	6 + 11	**34**	19 + 4	**35**	8 + 22
36	20 – 7 13	**37**	31 – 4	**38**	23 – 7	**39**	18 – 9	**40**	23 – 5

Exercise 8B

1	7 + 7	**2**	6 + 8	**3**	4 + 12	**4**	8 + 5	**5**	4 + 7
6	12 – 5	**7**	15 – 8	**8**	18 – 6	**9**	11 – 5	**10**	13 – 9
11	3 + 9	**12**	5 + 7	**13**	13 – 8	**14**	12 – 9	**15**	5 + 9
16	6 + 7	**17**	20 – 9	**18**	17 – 6	**19**	16 + 11	**20**	13 + 7
21	14 – 6	**22**	12 – 8	**23**	11 – 8	**24**	7 + 8	**25**	9 + 4
26	8 + 11	**27**	15 – 8	**28**	17 – 13	**29**	9 + 9	**30**	13 + 6
31	13 + 7	**32**	17 + 4	**33**	19 + 3	**34**	7 + 11	**35**	8 + 22
36	30 – 7	**37**	21 – 8	**38**	32 – 5	**39**	23 – 8	**40**	21 – 9

9/ MENTAL ARITHMETIC: ADDING AND SUBTRACTING TWO 2-DIGIT NUMBERS

There are many ways of doing these calculations in your head. One of the most common methods involves breaking one of the numbers into tens and units, and doing the calculation in two parts. Do *not* use a calculator.

> **EXAMPLE**
> ▶ 23 + 56 (remember 56 = 50 + 6)
>
> 23 + 50 = 73
> 73 + 6 = 79

▶ 45 − 13 (13 = 10 + 3)

    45 − 10 = 35
    35 − 3 = 32

Another 'trick' can be used when one of the numbers is nearly 10, 20, 30 and so on.

▶ 43 + 28

    28 is nearly 30: 43 + 30 = 73
    but it should have been +28: 73 − 2 = 71

▶ 65 − 19

    19 is nearly 20: 65 − 20 = 45
    but it was −19 not −20: 45 + 1 = 46

Exercise 9A

1	14 + 25	**2**	25 + 13	**3**	41 + 17	**4**	50 + 27	**5**	33 + 14
6	46 + 21	**7**	16 + 20	**8**	64 + 15	**9**	25 + 23	**10**	47 + 32
11	31 + 28	**12**	23 + 24	**13**	34 + 42	**14**	31 + 40	**15**	20 + 15
16	37 + 44	**17**	53 + 28	**18**	29 + 12	**19**	45 + 34	**20**	48 + 13
21	27 + 14	**22**	17 + 45	**23**	19 + 27	**24**	36 + 34	**25**	62 + 36
26	76 + 24	**27**	37 + 17	**28**	59 + 32	**29**	18 + 38	**30**	47 + 33
31	35 − 24	**32**	46 − 15	**33**	27 − 16	**34**	37 − 24	**35**	48 − 27
36	45 − 30	**37**	54 − 23	**38**	67 − 36	**39**	78 − 36	**40**	55 − 44

Exercise 9B

1	27 + 32	**2**	26 + 27	**3**	44 + 35	**4**	19 + 12	**5**	47 − 25
6	38 − 17	**7**	39 − 28	**8**	45 − 24	**9**	53 + 37	**10**	39 + 12
11	36 + 15	**12**	56 + 30	**13**	58 + 13	**14**	37 + 18	**15**	60 − 41
16	78 − 56	**17**	58 − 36	**18**	50 − 36	**19**	63 − 40	**20**	39 − 27
21	46 + 37	**22**	26 + 17	**23**	38 + 37	**24**	52 + 40	**25**	53 + 29
26	28 + 33	**27**	64 + 30	**28**	45 + 25	**29**	72 − 29	**30**	70 − 25
31	69 − 45	**32**	39 − 18	**33**	57 − 38	**34**	36 − 19	**35**	48 + 34
36	60 − 36	**37**	43 + 35	**38**	27 + 38	**39**	33 + 47	**40**	53 + 17

10/ MENTAL ARITHMETIC: ADDING AND SUBTRACTING SEVERAL 1-DIGIT NUMBERS

If there is a mixture of additions and subtractions, it is wiser to do the additions first. The subtractions can be done afterwards. Do *not* use a calculator.

EXAMPLE
▶ $5 - 7 + 8 + 3 - 4$
$$5 + 8 + 3 = 16$$
$$16 - 7 = 9$$
$$9 - 4 = 5$$

Exercise 10A

Do these in your head. That means no working should be written down and no calculators used.

1 $3 + 2 + 7$	**2** $6 + 9 + 5$	**3** $8 + 6 + 8$	**4** $4 + 9 + 5$
5 $9 + 6 + 5$	**6** $7 + 4 + 7$	**7** $2 + 5 + 6$	**8** $4 + 8 + 7$
9 $3 + 7 + 3$	**10** $8 + 9 + 5$	**11** $8 + 7 - 6$	**12** $6 + 5 - 3$
13 $4 - 3 + 7$	**14** $6 + 3 - 5$	**15** $1 - 8 + 9$	**16** $4 + 9 + 5$
17 $7 + 3 + 4$	**18** $8 + 9 - 7$	**19** $6 + 4 - 5$	**20** $8 + 6 - 3$

Exercise 10B

Do these in your head. That means no working should be written down and no calculators used.

1 $4 + 7 + 3$	**2** $2 + 6 + 5$	**3** $6 + 4 + 3$	**4** $9 + 7 + 4$
5 $3 + 5 + 8$	**6** $1 + 9 + 8$	**7** $8 + 5 + 3$	**8** $7 + 4 + 6$
9 $3 + 5 + 9$	**10** $5 + 6 + 2$	**11** $6 + 4 - 7$	**12** $7 + 8 - 3$
13 $5 + 8 - 6$	**14** $9 + 4 - 7$	**15** $8 - 6 + 3$	**16** $4 + 7 + 6$
17 $7 + 6 + 7$	**18** $4 - 7 + 8$	**19** $2 + 3 + 5$	**20** $5 + 6 - 8$

Exercise 10C

Do these in your head. That means no working should be written down and no calculators used.

1 $2 + 3 + 5 + 4$	**2** $6 + 4 + 2 + 8$	**3** $4 + 6 + 8 + 6$
4 $7 + 5 + 2 + 8$	**5** $3 + 8 + 7 + 3$	**6** $4 + 5 + 4 + 6 + 3$
7 $8 + 5 + 9 + 3 + 2$	**8** $3 + 4 + 6 + 2 + 8$	**9** $8 + 9 + 6 + 3 + 4$
10 $3 + 5 + 2 + 8 + 7$	**11** $3 + 8 - 2 + 5$	**12** $3 - 8 + 6 + 7$
13 $8 + 7 - 5 - 2$	**14** $9 + 7 - 2 - 4$	**15** $7 - 8 + 6 - 3$
16 $5 + 8 + 2 - 3 + 4$	**17** $6 - 8 + 5 + 3 - 4$	**18** $4 + 8 - 7 - 6 + 9 + 2$
19 $5 + 8 + 3 + 1 - 8 - 7$	**20** $6 + 4 + 6 + 8 - 7 - 6$	

Exercise 10D

Do these in your head. That means no working should be written down and no calculators used.

1	3 + 5 + 6 + 4	**2**	1 + 5 + 3 + 8	**3**	2 + 7 + 6 + 7
4	5 + 6 + 2 + 3	**5**	8 + 7 + 8 + 5	**6**	3 + 4 + 6 + 2 + 3
7	1 + 9 + 8 + 6 + 2	**8**	2 + 3 + 5 + 2 + 8	**9**	5 + 6 + 4 + 2 + 7
10	7 + 8 + 6 + 3 + 4	**11**	5 + 8 − 5 + 7	**12**	6 + 5 + 9 − 7
13	8 + 6 − 4 − 2	**14**	5 − 4 − 6 + 8	**15**	9 + 7 − 5 − 6
16	2 + 3 + 4 − 5 + 8	**17**	3 + 9 − 7 − 3 + 6	**18**	8 + 6 − 7 − 2 − 3 + 7
19	2 − 9 − 5 + 8 + 7 + 6	**20**	4 + 8 − 5 + 9 − 6 − 3		

11/ PROBLEMS INVOLVING SIMPLE ADDITION AND SUBTRACTION WITHOUT A CALCULATOR

It is wise to write down the arithmetic being used but you should do the calculations in your head. You must *not* use a calculator.

> **EXAMPLE**
>
> ► Tom has £13. He gives Mary £8. How much money does Tom have left?
>
> 13 − 8 = 5
> Tom has £5.

Exercise 11A

1 Gemma scores 8 on one test and 5 on another. What is her total mark in the two tests?

2 Dan cuts 6 metres of wire from a 15-metre roll. What length of wire is left?

3 What is the total value of an 8p and a 5p stamp?

4 Amber cycles 8 km before lunch and 9 km afterwards. How far did she cycle altogether?

5 Ian uses six exercise books in the first half of the year and eight books in the second half. How many books did he use in the year?

6 Kazi has seventeen rabbits. She sells eleven of them. How many does she have left?

7 Andrew was 9 years old in 1995. In which year was he born?

8 We have a total of nineteen light bulbs in our house. Five of these do not work. How many bulbs do work?

9 The scores on two dice are 6 and 5. What is the total score on the two dice?

10 Dominique grows twenty lettuces. She uses thirteen of them. How many lettuces remain?

11 How many days of my fifteen-day holiday remain after seven days?

12 The temperature is 16°C at noon but is only 7°C three hours later. By how many degrees has the temperature fallen?

13 Colin has eighteen litres of petrol at the start of a journey that uses nine litres. How many litres remain?

14 Mushar has nine zebra finches. He buys six more. How many zebra finches does Mushar have now?

15 Neil draws a line 7 cm long. He increases the length of the line to 19 cm. By how much does Neil increase the length of the line?

16 Wanderers score six goals in a game. They score eight in the next game. How many goals did they score in total in the two games?

17 Amelia has seven chairs in the lounge and nine in the dining room. How many chairs is this in total?

18 At the start of the day I have seventeen pages of a book left to read. I read nine pages. How many pages do I have left to read?

19 Etienne is laying sixteen patio slabs. He lays seven. How many slabs remain?

20 Phil buys eighteen eggs. He drops the box and breaks twelve eggs. How many eggs remain unbroken?

Exercise 11B

1 Luke uses six metres of foil from a 15-metre roll. What length is left?

2 Georgina's mother drives her 4 km to the station. Georgina completes her journey to school with a 9 km train ride. How far does she travel in total?

3 I take seventeen spoons to a dinner but can only find eight spoons to bring home. How many spoons did I lose?

4 Camilla has five litres of petrol. She buys twelve litres. How many litres does she have now?

5 At dawn the temperature is 7°C but at noon it is 19°C. By how much has the temperature risen during the morning?

6 A restaurant has thirteen tables in its main room and six in another room. How many tables are there in total?

7 Laurie buys 16 kg of apples at a market but finds that 7 kg need to be thrown away. How much does she have left?

8 A knife has a handle of length 8 cm and a blade of length 9 cm. How long is the knife altogether?

9 What is the date eleven days after 7 May.

10 Tracey has nineteen pet mice. She gives twelve to good homes. How many mice does she have left?

11 Russell has eleven tokens and collects six more. How many tokens does he have now?

12 Felix has seventeen chocolate eggs. He eats twelve. How many eggs are left?

13 Kathryn has twenty minutes to wait for her train. How much longer will she need to wait after thirteen minutes?

14 Rachel writes five pages on Monday. When she finishes writing on Tuesday, she has a total of eighteen pages. How many pages did she write on Tuesday?

15 A café starts the day with twenty litres of orange drink. At the end of the day eight litres remain. How many litres were used during the day?

16 Zak was born in 1982. How old is he in 1996?

17 Mika buys twenty envelopes. She uses thirteen of them. How many does she have left?

18 Penny scores 13 and 6 at darts. What is her total score?

19 In three games Rovers score sixteen goals. They score three goals in the first game and four in the second. How many goals did they score in the third game?

20 How long was Gail's holiday if she spent eight days staying in hotels and seven days camping?

Exercise 11C

1 Liz buys eighteen packets of crisps. She already has six packets. How many packets does she have altogether?

2 A café has twenty-five litres of milk. They use seventeen litres. How many litres remain?

3 Jason is paid for some work that he has done. He receives £9, £4 and £7. How much does he earn in total?

4 Katie has twenty-eight litres of petrol. She uses nineteen litres on a journey. How much petrol is left?

5 Stephen flies for fourteen hours in a plane, waits for five hours and flies for another eight hours. How long does his journey take?

6 David's train arrives at 12.14 p.m. and his next train leaves at 12.29 p.m. How many minutes does David have to wait?

7 In her last four matches Michelle scores seven, five, two and twelve points. What is her total for the four matches?

8 Simon requires twenty-five patio slabs. He has eighteen. How many more does he need?

9 Ed has eleven fishing floats; Karen has twelve. How many floats do they have between them?

10 Craig wants to buy a new iron costing £22. He has only £15. How much more money does he need?

11 A teacher opens a pack of twenty-four new books. He issues seventeen of these. How many books remain?

12 Gemma scores eight marks in her first test, seven marks on her second test and nine marks on her third test. What is her total for the three tests?

13 I have £25 at the start of the week. I spend £7, £5 and £6. How much money do I have left?

14 John has six pairs of socks and nine odd socks. How many socks does he have altogether?

15 A family go out for the day. Bus fares cost £6, snacks cost £12 and ice creams £6. What is the total cost?

16 Amy has twenty-eight pages left to read of her book. She reads sixteen pages. How many pages does she have left to read?

17 Stephen is allowed 20 kg of luggage. His case weighs 12 kg and his bag weighs 3 kg. How much more luggage can Stephen take?

18 Sam has twenty-two items to wash. He puts seventeen in the first wash. How many items remain?

19   Sarah is playing cards. She needs to add up the value of her five cards. She has a seven, a four, a three, a two and another two. What is the total value of her cards?

20   A family spent six days in France, five days in Spain and eight days in Portugal. How many days did they spend in total in the three countries?

Exercise 11D

1   Brian buys sixteen kilograms of potatoes but finds that he already has eight kilograms. How many kilograms does he have in total?

2   There are twenty-five butterflies on a bush. Nine fly away. How many are left?

3   Sehra was born in 1977. How old was she on her birthday in 1992?

4   Frank works seven hours on Monday, six hours on Tuesday and seven hours on Wednesday. How many hours did he work in total over the three days?

5   Terry has twenty-two pages of work to type. She has done eleven of them. How many pages are there left to type?

6   Ruth records the milk she buys during the week: three pints each day on Monday, Tuesday, Wednesday and Friday; two pints on Thursday; six pints on Saturday; and no milk on Sunday. How many pints of milk did she buy in the week?

7   Kirpal finds that she has twenty-eight pencils in her bag. She gives away twelve. How many pencils does she have now?

8   Richard scores thirteen marks in a test and eight marks in the next test. What is his total mark for the two tests?

9   Angelique arrives at the bus station at 11.13. She has to wait nine minutes for the bus. At what time did the bus arrive?

10   Adam has £23 but spends £8 and then £3. How much money does he have remaining?

11   The temperature at dawn is 13°C. By noon the temperature has risen by 11°C. What is the temperature at noon?

12   The total distance around a triangle is 29 cm. One of the sides measures 7 cm and another measures 9 cm. What is the length of the third side?

13   Angelo starts his holiday on 6 July and finishes on 21 July. How many days holiday did he have?

14   Kerry scores a total of nineteen points in two games. She scores seven points in her first game. How many points does she score in the second game?

15   Michelle has £13 in her wallet and £8 in her pocket. How much does she have in total?

16   Thomas cycles for 8 km, then for 7 km and finally for 9 km. How far did he cycle altogether?

17   I have fifteen litres of petrol. I buy seven litres. How many litres do I have now?

18   A tank contains twenty-six litres of water. Bill takes fifteen litres out of the tank. How many litres remain?

19   Jaspal buys a packet of five washers. She already has eighteen washers. How many does she have in total?

20   A journey takes twenty-one hours. After twelve hours how many hours remain?

12/ ADDING AND SUBTRACTING TWO 3-DIGIT NUMBERS WITHOUT A CALCULATOR

It is important to set these calculations in straight columns. If the numbers are untidy and the columns are not straight, it makes the work so much more difficult. Show clearly the numbers that are carried forward.

EXAMPLE
▶ 245 + 587

```
  2 4 5
  5 8 7
  8 3 2
  1 1
```

EXAMPLE
▶ 500 – 342

```
  ⁴ ⁹ ¹
  5 1̸0̸ 0̸
  3 4 2
  1 5 8
```

Exercise 12A

1	107 + 362	**2**	316 + 213	**3**	624 + 332	**4**	501 + 142
5	244 + 326	**6**	433 + 58	**7**	215 + 376	**8**	624 – 313
9	487 – 235	**10**	594 – 354	**11**	276 – 136	**12**	357 – 138
13	811 – 420	**14**	719 – 44	**15**	235 + 215	**16**	384 – 185
17	537 + 425	**18**	608 – 366	**19**	247 + 66	**20**	401 – 299

Exercise 12B

1	204 + 155	**2**	326 + 242	**3**	513 + 126	**4**	426 + 332
5	514 + 66	**6**	365 + 215	**7**	482 + 218	**8**	485 – 234
9	557 – 342	**10**	643 – 235	**11**	337 – 95	**12**	412 – 103
13	811 – 420	**14**	747 – 358	**15**	364 + 263	**16**	600 – 89
17	277 + 285	**18**	506 – 324	**19**	409 + 376	**20**	253 – 199

Exercise 12C

1	278 + 367	**2**	166 + 379	**3**	382 + 519	**4**	409 + 249
5	264 + 44	**6**	775 + 155	**7**	407 + 394	**8**	342 – 161
9	509 – 27	**10**	624 – 443	**11**	800 – 325	**12**	503 – 375
13	203 – 98	**14**	458 – 186	**15**	103+ 205 + 88	**16**	305 + 176 + 263
17	205 + 178 – 155	**18**	507 + 248 – 277	**19**	343 + 178 + 209	**20**	407 – 199 + 257

Exercise 12D

1 203 + 588	**2** 326 + 157	**3** 628 + 162	**4** 47 + 153
5 263 + 127	**6** 608 + 156	**7** 465 + 207	**8** 521 − 207
9 427 − 251	**10** 623 − 332	**11** 708 − 213	**12** 562 − 95
13 966 − 438	**14** 305 − 184	**15** 132 + 214 + 358	**16** 45 + 109 + 217
17 542 + 154 − 205	**18** 618 + 287 − 524	**19** 387 + 119 − 257	**20** 189 − 265 + 564

13/ MULTIPLICATION TABLES

It is essential to know the multiplication tables. You do not know them properly if you need to say $2 \times 6 = 12$, $3 \times 6 = 18$, $4 \times 6 = 24$, and so 5×6 must be 30. You must know *immediately* that $5 \times 6 = 30$.
There are lots of examples below.

Exercise 13A

Test 1

1 4×3 = 12	**2** 5×4 = 20
3 3×3 = 9	**4** 5×3 = 15
5 2×1 = 2	**6** 4×5 = 20
7 3×4 = 12	**8** 2×3 = 6
9 3×5 = 15	**10** 4×4 = 16
11 2×5 = 10	**12** 6×4 = 24
13 5×5 = 25	**14** 2×6 = 12
15 3×7 = 21	**16** 6×0 = 0
17 4×7 = 28	**18** 3×6 = 18
19 6×5 = 30	**20** 2×7 = 14

Test 2

1 2×9 = 18	**2** 7×3 = 21
3 3×1 = 3	**4** 2×10 = 20
5 4×6 = 24	**6** 3×8 = 24
7 3×10 = 30	**8** 5×6 = 30
9 7×5 = 35	**10** 6×10 = 60
11 4×3 = 12	**12** 2×5 = 10
13 4×7 = 28	**14** 5×0 = 0
15 4×4 = 16	**16** 2×7 = 14
17 6×3 = 18	**18** 4×10 = 40
19 3×5 = 15	**20** 3×3 = 9

Test 3

1 2×4 = 8	**2** 4×5 = 20
3 3×7 = 21	**4** 5×10 = 50
5 2×9 = 18	**6** 3×4 = 12
7 2×3 = 6	**8** 5×0 = 0
9 6×4 = 24	**10** 7×3 = 21
11 3×10 = 30	**12** 2×6 = 12
13 5×4 = 20	**14** 4×3 = 12
15 $5 \times$ 15	**16** 3×9 = 27
17 2×10 = 20	**18** 4×6 = 24
19 3×4 = 12	**20** 5×3 = 15

Test 4

1 4×5	**2** 3×7
3 2×4	**4** 3×10
5 2×9	**6** 3×3
7 2×5	**8** 3×4
9 4×3	**10** 2×7
11 5×10	**12** 2×3
13 3×5	**14** 5×4
15 2×6	**16** 2×8
17 4×10	**18** 4×4
19 5×5	**20** 3×9

Test 5

1 3×6	**2** 2×10
3 3×3	**4** 2×5
5 3×10	**6** 2×4
7 3×5	**8** 4×3
9 2×7	**10** 4×10
11 5×3	**12** 4×4
13 3×7	**14** 5×4
15 2×10	**16** 2×9
17 6×3	**18** 4×5
19 2×8	**20** 3×4

Test 6

1 4×3	**2** 2×5
3 5×3	**4** 2×4
5 3×5	**6** 2×3
7 3×4	**8** 3×3
9 5×5	**10** 4×4
11 4×5	**12** 3×10
13 5×4	**14** 3×3
15 2×4	**16** 3×5
17 4×3	**18** 5×4
19 2×5	**20** 3×10

Test 7

1	5×3	**2**	3×4
3	2×3	**4**	4×5
5	2×6	**6**	4×10
7	4×4	**8**	5×5
9	3×6	**10**	2×7
11	5×10	**12**	3×3
13	4×5	**14**	2×4
15	3×10	**16**	2×3
17	3×5	**18**	4×4
19	5×3	**20**	4×10

Test 8

1	2×5	**2**	4×3
3	5×5	**4**	2×6
5	3×4	**6**	5×10
7	2×7	**8**	5×4
9	2×9	**10**	6×10
11	5×3	**12**	2×6
13	3×10	**14**	3×5
15	2×7	**16**	3×4
17	2×3	**18**	4×5
19	2×4	**20**	4×10

Exercise 13B

Test 1

1	4×3	**2**	3×7
3	2×4	**4**	3×5
5	2×3	**6**	4×4
7	3×6	**8**	4×5
9	3×0	**10**	5×4
11	2×6	**12**	5×5
13	2×8	**14**	5×3
15	2×9	**16**	3×8
17	2×0	**18**	6×4
19	2×5	**20**	3×4

Test 2

1	6×3	**2**	3×9
3	4×10	**4**	4×0
5	5×6	**6**	7×4
7	4×9	**8**	6×10
9	4×8	**10**	6×5
11	5×3	**12**	4×5
13	3×7	**14**	2×9
15	5×10	**16**	3×4
17	2×6	**18**	3×5
19	4×1	**20**	5×4

Test 3

1	3×9	**2**	2×7
3	2×5	**4**	3×3
5	2×0	**6**	4×7
7	3×10	**8**	4×4
9	3×6	**10**	5×5
11	5×3	**12**	3×7
13	4×4	**14**	4×6
15	6×7	**16**	3×9
17	6×10	**18**	3×1
19	4×5	**20**	5×6

Test 4

1	4×3	**2**	5×4
3	3×6	**4**	4×7
5	2×9	**6**	3×10
7	6×3	**8**	2×7
9	3×5	**10**	2×6
11	6×5	**12**	4×9
13	7×10	**14**	4×8
15	6×6	**16**	2×4
17	5×5	**18**	8×7
19	5×9	**20**	6×8

Test 5

1	7×6	**2**	8×5
3	7×7	**4**	8×3
5	10×4	**6**	9×5
7	7×9	**8**	5×7
9	2×8	**10**	7×5
11	7×8	**12**	10×5
13	9×7	**14**	6×9
15	8×6	**16**	9×9
17	9×3	**18**	8×8
19	6×4	**20**	5×8

Test 6

1	5×3	**2**	4×8
3	6×9	**4**	3×5
5	7×8	**6**	3×9
7	5×4	**8**	7×5
9	6×8	**10**	5×6
11	8×3	**12**	3×3
13	8×7	**14**	7×9
15	5×8	**16**	6×6
17	7×4	**18**	6×3
19	5×5	**20**	6×7

TEST 7

1	2×8	**2**	3×7
3	9×5	**4**	10×5
5	4×6	**6**	8×9
7	7×3	**8**	6×4
9	3×6	**10**	5×7
11	4×9	**12**	9×3
13	10×4	**14**	7×7
15	6×5	**16**	4×3
17	5×9	**18**	9×7
19	8×6	**20**	4×4

TEST 8

1	2×7	**2**	8×5
3	3×4	**4**	8×8
5	4×7	**6**	2×9
7	7×10	**8**	7×6
9	4×5	**10**	3×8
11	9×4	**12**	5×5
13	9×8	**14**	8×4
15	9×6	**16**	6×10
17	9×9	**18**	6×3
19	8×5	**20**	4×7

14/ DIVISIBILITY

There are some easy rules to see if a number can be divided exactly.

Divides by	Rule
2	Even number: ends in 0, 2, 4, 6, 8
3	Add up digits: if total of digits divides by 3, so does the number itself
4	Look at last two digits: if the number they make divides by 4, so does the number itself
5	Ends in 5 or 0
6	Even number *and* divides by 3
7	No rule
8	Look at last three digits: if the number they make divides by 8, so does the number itself
9	Add up digits: if total of digits divides by 9, so does the number itself
10	Ends in 0

EXAMPLE

▶ Check 3465 for divisibility by 2, 5 and 10.

3465 is *not* divisible by 2
3465 is divisible by 5 (ends in 5)
3465 is *not* divisible by 10.

So 3465 is divisible by 5.

▶ Check 214 632 for divisibility by the numbers from 2 to 10.

divisible by 2 (even)
divisible by 3 (digit total = 18)
divisible by 4 (32 divides by 4)
not divisible by 5
divisible by 6 (even and divides by 3)
not divisible by 7 (try it)
divisible by 8 (632 divides by 8)
divisible by 9 (digit total = 18)
not divisible by 10

So 214 632 is divisible by 2, 3, 4, 6, 8 and 9.

Exercise 14A

State whether each of the following is divisible by 2, 5 and 10.

1	230	**2**	125	**3**	226	**4**	150	**5**	344
6	345	**7**	723	**8**	605	**9**	506	**10**	220
11	225	**12**	427	**13**	428	**14**	510	**15**	321
16	435	**17**	440	**18**	259	**19**	119	**20**	560

Exercise 14B

State whether each of the following is divisible by 2, 5 and 10.

1	595	**2**	670	**3**	548	**4**	512	**5**	685
6	705	**7**	583	**8**	735	**9**	650	**10**	240
11	285	**12**	437	**13**	445	**14**	799	**15**	800
16	205	**17**	365	**18**	386	**19**	486	**20**	485

Exercise 14C

State whether each of the following is divisible by 2, 3, 4, 5, 6, 7, 8, 9 and 10.

1	2106	**2**	2160	**3**	7685	**4**	5148	**5**	1784
6	1022	**7**	2875	**8**	4140	**9**	3333	**10**	5285
11	8344	**12**	8114	**13**	689	**14**	4105	**15**	2560
16	4014	**17**	9738	**18**	529	**19**	3036	**20**	4536

Exercise 14D

State whether each of the following is divisible by 2, 3, 4, 5, 6, 7, 8, 9 and 10.

1	2892	**2**	1701	**3**	5102	**4**	7010	**5**	6344
6	1636	**7**	4500	**8**	5329	**9**	3261	**10**	5538
11	8124	**12**	1161	**13**	3128	**14**	4081	**15**	4908
16	9885	**17**	9192	**18**	1341	**19**	1344	**20**	2444

15/ DIVISION: TIMES TABLES IN REVERSE

Exercise 15A

1	21 ÷ 3	**2**	25 ÷ 5	**3**	20 ÷ 4	**4**	16 ÷ 2	**5**	30 ÷ 5
6	12 ÷ 3	**7**	24 ÷ 4	**8**	6 ÷ 2	**9**	8 ÷ 4	**10**	20 ÷ 5
11	24 ÷ 3	**12**	14 ÷ 2	**13**	15 ÷ 5	**14**	18 ÷ 3	**15**	10 ÷ 5
16	12 ÷ 2	**17**	9 ÷ 3	**18**	28 ÷ 4	**19**	40 ÷ 5	**20**	10 ÷ 2
21	20 ÷ 2	**22**	15 ÷ 3	**23**	16 ÷ 4	**24**	35 ÷ 5	**25**	18 ÷ 2
26	30 ÷ 3	**27**	32 ÷ 4	**28**	27 ÷ 3	**29**	12 ÷ 4	**30**	45 ÷ 5

Exercise 15B

1	20 ÷ 5	**2**	12 ÷ 3	**3**	14 ÷ 2	**4**	21 ÷ 3	**5**	28 ÷ 4
6	30 ÷ 5	**7**	12 ÷ 2	**8**	25 ÷ 5	**9**	24 ÷ 3	**10**	20 ÷ 2
11	20 ÷ 4	**12**	10 ÷ 2	**13**	9 ÷ 3	**14**	12 ÷ 4	**15**	45 ÷ 5
16	27 ÷ 3	**17**	16 ÷ 2	**18**	16 ÷ 4	**19**	15 ÷ 3	**20**	10 ÷ 5
21	40 ÷ 4	**22**	15 ÷ 5	**23**	24 ÷ 4	**24**	18 ÷ 3	**25**	18 ÷ 2
26	40 ÷ 5	**27**	35 ÷ 5	**28**	36 ÷ 4	**29**	32 ÷ 4	**30**	30 ÷ 3

Exercise 15C

1	45 ÷ 9	**2**	24 ÷ 3	**3**	45 ÷ 5	**4**	28 ÷ 4	**5**	18 ÷ 2
6	24 ÷ 8	**7**	35 ÷ 5	**8**	28 ÷ 7	**9**	32 ÷ 8	**10**	80 ÷ 10
11	36 ÷ 9	**12**	49 ÷ 7	**13**	27 ÷ 3	**14**	24 ÷ 4	**15**	40 ÷ 5
16	48 ÷ 8	**17**	54 ÷ 9	**18**	40 ÷ 8	**19**	56 ÷ 7	**20**	72 ÷ 9
21	42 ÷ 6	**22**	36 ÷ 4	**23**	25 ÷ 5	**24**	42 ÷ 7	**25**	27 ÷ 9
26	36 ÷ 6	**27**	56 ÷ 8	**28**	35 ÷ 7	**29**	64 ÷ 8	**30**	48 ÷ 6

1	27 ÷ 9	**2**	24 ÷ 3	**3**	42 ÷ 7	**4**	24 ÷ 8	**5**	48 ÷ 8
6	30 ÷ 6	**7**	45 ÷ 5	**8**	56 ÷ 7	**9**	45 ÷ 9	**10**	64 ÷ 8
11	42 ÷ 6	**12**	36 ÷ 4	**13**	72 ÷ 8	**14**	63 ÷ 9	**15**	49 ÷ 7
16	36 ÷ 6	**17**	30 ÷ 5	**18**	32 ÷ 8	**19**	54 ÷ 9	**20**	56 ÷ 8
21	54 ÷ 6	**22**	32 ÷ 4	**23**	72 ÷ 9	**24**	63 ÷ 7	**25**	81 ÷ 9
26	35 ÷ 7	**27**	48 ÷ 6	**28**	36 ÷ 9	**29**	28 ÷ 7	**30**	40 ÷ 8

16/ SIMPLE NUMBER FACTORS

If two numbers are multiplied together to give an answer of 20, there are several possible choices. There is 2 × 10 and 4 × 5 but 5 × 4 and 10 × 2 also work. (There is 1 × 20 or 20 × 1 as well but do not be use this type in these exercises.)

> **EXAMPLE**
> ▶ Write two examples of a pair of factors that can be multiplied together to give 24. Do not use 1 × 24 as an example. Choose *different* numbers for your second example.
>
> 6 × 4 = 24 and 3 × 8 = 24 (Note: You could also have used 2 × 12.)

Write down *one* example of a pair of factors which can be multiplied together to give each of the following numbers.
Do *not* use 1 as a factor.

1	6	**2**	12	**3**	4	**4**	14	**5**	21
6	24	**7**	22	**8**	15	**9**	8	**10**	121
11	49	**12**	35	**13**	52	**14**	80	**15**	25
16	30	**17**	27	**18**	42	**19**	32	**20**	20
21	28	**22**	56	**23**	45	**24**	50	**25**	63
26	48	**27**	40	**28**	72	**29**	54	**30**	60

Write down *one* example of a pair of factors which can be multiplied together to give each of the following numbers.
Do *not* use 1 as a factor.

1	10	**2**	18	**3**	26	**4**	9	**5**	21
6	16	**7**	85	**8**	39	**9**	35	**10**	38

11	46	**12**	51	**13**	99	**14**	65	**15**	42
16	125	**17**	33	**18**	34	**19**	66	**20**	75
21	98	**22**	100	**23**	90	**24**	200	**25**	36
26	81	**27**	84	**28**	44	**29**	64	**30**	120

Exercise 16C

(This can be used as an alternative to or as revision of Exercise 16A.)

Write down *two* examples (where possible) of a pair of factors which can be multiplied together to give each of the numbers in Exercise 16A. Do not make your second example the reverse of your first example (that is *not* 7 × 8 with 8 × 7).
Do *not* use 1 as a factor.

Exercise 16D

(This can be used as an alternative to or as revision of Exercise 16B.)

Write down *two* examples (where possible) of a pair of factors which can be multiplied together to give each of the numbers in Exercise 16B. Do not make your second example the reverse of your first example (that is *not* 7 × 8 with 8 × 7).
Do *not* use 1 as a factor.

17/ MULTIPLICATION AND DIVISION BY A SINGLE-DIGIT NUMBER WITHOUT A CALCULATOR

Exercise 17A

1	32 × 5	**2**	48 ÷ 2	**3**	36 ÷ 3	**4**	34 × 5	**5**	45 × 2
6	84 ÷ 4	**7**	24 × 5	**8**	75 ÷ 5	**9**	41 × 3	**10**	26 × 2
11	95 ÷ 5	**12**	36 ÷ 2	**13**	64 × 4	**14**	75 ÷ 3	**15**	35 × 4
16	90 ÷ 3	**17**	23 × 5	**18**	74 ÷ 2	**19**	61 × 4	**20**	52 ÷ 4

Exercise 17B

1	43 × 3	**2**	85 ÷ 5	**3**	24 × 4	**4**	62 × 5	**5**	34 × 2
6	88 ÷ 4	**7**	43 × 2	**8**	84 ÷ 3	**9**	51 × 5	**10**	48 ÷ 4
11	93 ÷ 3	**12**	47 × 2	**13**	95 ÷ 5	**14**	37 × 3	**15**	96 ÷ 4
16	27 × 3	**17**	92 ÷ 2	**18**	45 × 4	**19**	78 ÷ 3	**20**	65 ÷ 5

Exercise 17C

1	49 × 6	**2**	39 × 5	**3**	96 ÷ 6	**4**	47 × 8	**5**	795 ÷ 5
6	43 × 7	**7**	63 × 6	**8**	224 ÷ 7	**9**	36 × 5	**10**	171 ÷ 9
11	882 ÷ 6	**12**	18 × 9	**13**	38 × 8	**14**	686 ÷ 7	**15**	72 × 7
16	738 ÷ 9	**17**	744 ÷ 8	**18**	83 × 9	**19**	872 ÷ 8	**20**	59 × 5

Exercise 17D

1	75 × 6	**2**	225 ÷ 5	**3**	47 × 9	**4**	720 ÷ 6	**5**	89 × 8
6	840 ÷ 7	**7**	57 × 5	**8**	53 × 6	**9**	86 × 5	**10**	558 ÷ 6
11	854 ÷ 7	**12**	53 × 9	**13**	672 ÷ 8	**14**	66 × 7	**15**	875 ÷ 5
16	288 ÷ 9	**17**	98 × 8	**18**	77 × 7	**19**	736 ÷ 8	**20**	477 ÷ 9

18/ MULTIPLYING AND DIVIDING BY 10,100 AND 1000

To multiply by 10, add a zero.
To multiply by 100, add two zeros.

To divide by 10, cross off a zero.
To divide by 100, cross off two zeros

EXAMPLES

▶ 123 × 10 = 1230
123 × 100 = 12 300
67 × 1000 = 67 000

1230 ÷ 10 = 123
12 300 ÷ 100 = 123
67 000 ÷ 100 = 670

Exercise 18A

1	12 × 10	**2**	65 × 100	**3**	32 000 ÷ 100	**4**	600 ÷ 10
5	453 × 100	**6**	56 × 10	**7**	74 500 ÷ 100	**8**	23 000 ÷ 1000
9	253 × 10	**10**	85 × 100	**11**	94 000 ÷ 1000	**12**	3500 ÷ 10
13	17 × 1000	**14**	5970 × 100	**15**	945 × 10	**16**	67 000 ÷ 1000
17	80 900 ÷ 100	**18**	7500 ÷ 10	**19**	109 × 100	**20**	88 × 10
21	4120 × 10	**22**	4000 ÷ 100	**23**	90 000 ÷ 1000	**24**	430 ÷ 10
25	197 × 100	**26**	5 × 1000	**27**	690 × 100	**28**	84 000 ÷ 1000
29	5500 ÷ 10	**30**	940 000 ÷ 100				

1. 41×100
2. 76×10
3. 52×1000
4. $4500 \div 10$
5. $7200 \div 100$
6. $18\,000 \div 1000$
7. 487×10
8. 809×100
9. 6721×10
10. $9600 \div 10$
11. $70\,000 \div 1000$
12. 19×1000
13. 300×100
14. 870×10
15. $5960 \div 10$
16. $71\,000 \div 1000$
17. $82\,000 \div 100$
18. 282×10
19. 11×1000
20. 110×100
21. $1010 \div 10$
22. $43\,000 \div 100$
23. $67\,000 \div 1000$
24. $8500 \div 10$
25. 680×100
26. 86×100
27. 3×1000
28. $32\,000 \div 100$
29. $6100 \div 100$
30. $57\,000 \div 10$

REVISION

Exercise A

1. Write the following in words:
   two thousand, five hundred and
   two(2)million, five sixty seven
   a thousandand an
   (a) 607   (b) 2567   (c) 52 125   (d) 2 005 650
   fiftytwo thousand, one hundred and 25
   six hundred and seven

2. Write the following in numbers:
   (a) one hundred and thirty-six 136   2527 (b) two thousand, five hundred and twenty-seven
   (c) forty thousand, six hundred and twelve   (d) two hundred and seven thousand, and fifty

3. State, in words, the value of each digit that is underlined in the following:
   40,612   270,50
   (a) 48_3_   (b) 2_7_15   (c) 3_4_ 239   (d) _1_06 743

4. Place the numbers in order of size, smallest first:
   (a) 67, 95, 45, 56, 78   (b) 236, 198, 455, 623, 191
   (c) 4026, 701, 2403, 3994, 3746   (d) 2354, 2534, 3245, 3425, 2345

5. Convert to pounds:
   (a) 107p £1.07 (b) 325p £3.25 (c) 3025p £30.25 (d) 85p £0.85

6. Convert to pence:
   (a) £1.35 135p (b) £0.97 97p (c) £10.67 1067p (d) £32.18 3218p

7. (a) £3.28 + £5.85 9.13 (b) £11.05 – £9.56 £1.49 1067p

8. (a) 15 + 5 20.13 (b) 13 – 8 5 (c) 9 + 6 15 (d) 16 – 7 9 (e) 8 + 8 16
   (f) 24 – 9 15 (g) 31 – 8 23 (h) 27 + 4 31 (i) 35 + 7 42 (j) 42 – 5 37

9. (a) 22 + 17 39 (b) 26 – 13 13 (c) 32 + 28 60 (d) 56 – 29 27 (e) 75 + 16 91
   (f) 44 – 28 16 (g) 37 + 48 87 (h) 81 – 69 12 (i) 53 + 45 98 (j) 63 – 36 27

10. (a) 2 + 6 – 3 5 (b) 9 – 7 + 5 7 (c) 6 + 4 + 2 – 3 9 (d) 8 + 7 – 5 + 1 11
    (e) 6 + 5 – 9 +3 5 (f) 6 – 8 + 2 + 3 3 (g) 5 + 3 + 7 – 4 11 (h) 7 + 7 – 8 – 4 2

11. (a) 245 + 618 863 (b) 376 – 157 219 (c) 419 + 383 802 (d) 700 – 372 328 (e) 444 + 266

12. (a) 2 × 9 18 (b) 7 × 4 28 (c) 6 × 3 18 (d) 5 × 8 40 (e) 8 × 7 56
    (f) 4 × 6 24 (g) 6 × 7 42 (h) 7 × 5 35 (i) 8 × 6 48 (j) 5 × 9 45

13. Check these numbers for divisibility by 2, 5 and 10:
    (a) 150 2   (b) 444 2
    5
    10

$\times \dfrac{75}{8} = 600$

14 Check these numbers for divisibility by 2, 3, 4, 5, 6, 7, 8, 9 and 10:
   (a) 6213 6 9   (b) 3500 2 4 5 10

15 (a) 24 ÷ 3 8   (b) 20 ÷ 4 5   (c) 30 ÷ 6 5   (d) 30 ÷ 5 6   (e) 27 ÷ 9 3
   (f) 56 ÷ 7 8   (g) 36 ÷ 6 6   (h) 63 ÷ 9 7   (i) 40 ÷ 8 5   (j) 54 ÷ 6 9

16 Write down *two* examples (where possible) of a pair of factors which can be multiplied together to give each of the following the numbers. Do *not* use 1 as a factor.
   (a) 20 5×4   (b) 42 7×6   (c) 35 7×5   (d) 72 8×9   (e) 49 7
   2×10   24×2   36×2   37

17 (a) 17 ×10 170   (b) 260 ÷ 10 26   (c) 3000 ÷ 100 30   (d) 5 × 1000 5000   (e) 3700 ÷ 100 37
   (f) 201 × 10   (g) 71 000 ÷ 10   (h) 604 × 100   (i) 9000 ÷ 10   (j) 87 × 10 000
   2010   7100   60400   900   8700000 60

6
12
18
24
30
36
42
48
54
54

Exercise AA

1 Thirty-three thousand, eight hundred and ten people passed through the turnstiles at a sporting event. Write this in number form.   33,810

2 The population of South Korea is approximately forty-two million, two hundred thousand. Write this in number form.   42,200,000

3 Mansoora has 12 435 plastic spoons to put into packets of 100. How many complete packets will she be able to fill?   124

4 The digits 3, 1, 7 and 9 are each used once to make four-figure numbers. State (a) the largest possible number and (b) the smallest possible number that can be made from these digits.   a) 9731   b) 1379

5 Mark has a £10 note. He buys items costing £2.95, £1.35, £1.05, £2.18 and £0.99. How much change does he receive?   £1.48

6 Sally is counting the coins that she has collected from her market stall. She has twelve £1 coins, thirty-five 10p coins, twenty 2p coins and eighteen 1p coins. How much money does she have in total?   £16.08

7 Dianne counts the cars in the car park. There are five red, six white, four grey and seven of other colours. How many cars are there in total?   22

8 Harry walks 4 km to Terry's house and then 3 km into town. He walks 5 km home by a direct route. How far does he walk altogether?   12 km

9 The temperature is 8°C now but it was 15°C earlier. By how much has the temperature dropped?   7°C

10 Helen buys a packet of 25 envelopes. She uses 16 of them. How many does she have left?   9

11 Roger has 7 litres of petrol. He buys another 16 litres. How much petrol does he have now?   23L

12 Ann has five packets of card. Each packet has eight sheets. If she needs thirty-five sheets, how many sheets does she have left over?   5

13 Keith scores 67 playing a game but loses 29 points for breaking the rules. How many points does he have now?   38 points

14 Six people share £78 equally. How much does each receive?   13

15 There are 235 packets of biscuits on the shelf of a supermarket. If there are another 144 packets in the store, how many packets are there altogether?

16 There are 236 Year 11 students at a school. If 157 leave at the end of the year, how many are left?

17 Two numbers multiplied together make 36. State two *pairs* of suitable numbers.

18 The number 13 453 does not divide by 6 or 9. State the next higher number that divides by (a) 6 (b) 9.

19 There are 125 labels in a packet. How many labels are there in eight packets?

20 One section of fencing measures 95 cm. What is the length, in centimetres, of ten sections.

19/ DIVISION TO THE NEAREST WHOLE NUMBER WITH OR WITHOUT A CALCULATOR

When a number is divided, the answer is not necessarily a whole number. When a calculator is used, the answer is often a decimal. Without a calculator there is often a remainder.

These exercises are about dividing and then knowing whether to **round up** or **round down** to the nearest whole number.

Without a calculator

EXAMPLE

▶ $59 \div 7 = 8$ remainder 3
$= 8$ to the nearest whole number.

The remainder of 3 is less than half of the number used for dividing (7), so round *down* to 8.

EXAMPLE

▶ $77 \div 8 = 9$ remainder 5
$= 10$ to the nearest whole number.

The remainder of 5 is more than half of the number used for dividing (8), so round *up* to 10.

With a calculator

EXAMPLE

▶ $52 \div 7 = 7.428$
$= 7$ to the nearest whole number.

7.5 is halfway between 7 and 8; 7.428 is less than 7.5 so round *down* to 7.

EXAMPLE

▶ $76 \div 8 = 9.5$
$= 10$ to the nearest whole number.

If the number is exactly halfway between two numbers, always round *up*.

Exercise 19A

Give the answers to these division questions to the nearest whole number.
(These questions are suitable for mental arithmetic.)

1	21 ÷ 5	**2**	31 ÷ 3	**3**	43 ÷ 4	**4**	27 ÷ 6	**5**	37 ÷ 4
6	25 ÷ 3	**7**	34 ÷ 5	**8**	62 ÷ 3	**9**	26 ÷ 4	**10**	27 ÷ 5
11	43 ÷ 5	**12**	67 ÷ 4	**13**	25 ÷ 4	**14**	82 ÷ 5	**15**	29 ÷ 6
16	50 ÷ 4	**17**	42 ÷ 5	**18**	20 ÷ 3	**19**	45 ÷ 6	**20**	58 ÷ 3

Exercise 19B

Give the answers to these division questions to the nearest whole number.
(These questions are suitable for mental arithmetic.)

1	13 ÷ 3	**2**	18 ÷ 4	**3**	17 ÷ 5	**4**	19 ÷ 6	**5**	13 ÷ 5
6	65 ÷ 3	**7**	46 ÷ 3	**8**	22 ÷ 4	**9**	43 ÷ 6	**10**	39 ÷ 6
11	46 ÷ 5	**12**	63 ÷ 4	**13**	23 ÷ 5	**14**	33 ÷ 6	**15**	47 ÷ 3
16	53 ÷ 4	**17**	61 ÷ 5	**18**	17 ÷ 3	**19**	22 ÷ 5	**20**	25 ÷ 4

Exercise 19C

Give the answers to these division questions to the nearest whole number.
(These questions are suitable for mental arithmetic or a calculator.)

1	141 ÷ 6	**2**	338 ÷ 9	**3**	260 ÷ 8	**4**	767 ÷ 9	**5**	434 ÷ 7
6	135 ÷ 8	**7**	889 ÷ 7	**8**	369 ÷ 6	**9**	148 ÷ 9	**10**	483 ÷ 9
11	644 ÷ 8	**12**	354 ÷ 8	**13**	151 ÷ 9	**14**	590 ÷ 7	**15**	674 ÷ 8
16	371 ÷ 6	**17**	986 ÷ 8	**18**	145 ÷ 7	**19**	235 ÷ 6	**20**	477 ÷ 8

Exercise 19D

Give the answers to these division questions to the nearest whole number.
(These questions are suitable for mental arithmetic or a calculator.)

1	668 ÷ 5	**2**	368 ÷ 7	**3**	268 ÷ 9	**4**	936 ÷ 8	**5**	160 ÷ 7
6	237 ÷ 7	**7**	342 ÷ 8	**8**	761 ÷ 9	**9**	369 ÷ 8	**10**	239 ÷ 7
11	530 ÷ 9	**12**	751 ÷ 8	**13**	463 ÷ 6	**14**	368 ÷ 6	**15**	865 ÷ 7
16	892 ÷ 8	**17**	161 ÷ 8	**18**	733 ÷ 9	**19**	243 ÷ 8	**20**	581 ÷ 6

20/ APPROXIMATING TO THE NEAREST 10 OR 100

Approximating to the nearest 10

Numbers ending in 4 and below round *down*. Numbers ending in 5 and above round *up*.

For example, 134 = 130 (to the nearest 10),
but 135 = 140 (to the nearest 10).

Approximating to the nearest 100

Numbers ending in 49 and below round *down*. Numbers ending in 50 and above round *up*.

For example, 349 = 300 (to the nearest 100),
but 350 = 400 (to the nearest 100).

Exercise 20A

Approximate each number to the nearest 10 or nearest 100 as indicated.

Nearest 10

1	27	**2**	54	**3**	42	**4**	38	**5**	69
6	96	**7**	81	**8**	18	**9**	25	**10**	44

Nearest 100

11	125	**12**	154	**13**	148	**14**	189	**15**	321
16	276	**17**	309	**18**	351	**19**	439	**20**	562

(a) Nearest 10 (b) Nearest 100

21	75	**22**	626	**23**	648	**24**	721	**25**	745
26	754	**27**	915	**28**	837	**29**	861	**30**	555

Exercise 20B

Approximate each number to the nearest 10 or nearest 100 as indicated.

Nearest 10

1	31	**2**	37	**3**	44	**4**	45	**5**	67
6	72	**7**	89	**8**	74	**9**	65	**10**	79

Nearest 100

11	235	**12**	467	**13**	349	**14**	350	**15**	219
16	409	**17**	569	**18**	551	**19**	742	**20**	609

(a) Nearest 10 (b) Nearest 100

21	89	**22**	542	**23**	849	**24**	853	**25**	901
26	979	**27**	827	**28**	765	**29**	450	**30**	354

21/ ESTIMATING THE ANSWERS TO ADDITIONS AND SUBTRACTIONS

EXAMPLE

▶ Estimate the answer to 143 + 259 and then add the two numbers to see if the estimation was good.

143 is approximately 140 and 259 is approximately 260.
So the answer is approximately 140 + 260 = 400.

$$\begin{array}{r} 143 \\ +259 \\ \hline 402 \end{array}$$

The exact answer is 402 so the approximation was good.

EXAMPLE

▶ Estimate the answer to 67 + 79.

This is approximately 70 + 80 = 150.

EXAMPLE

▶ By approximating to the nearest 100, estimate the answer to 327 − 239.

This is approximately 300 − 200 = 100.

Exercise 21A

In each of the following questions:
(a) Estimate the answer by approximating the numbers to the nearest 10.
(b) Complete the calculation and compare your answer with your estimate.

1 68 + 73	**2** 43 + 29	**3** 57 + 85	**4** 176 − 78	**5** 95 + 24
6 54 + 221	**7** 146 − 52	**8** 82 − 57	**9** 185 − 38	**10** 129 + 42

In each of the following questions:
(a) Estimate the answer by approximating the numbers to the nearest 100.
(b) Complete the calculation and compare your answer with your estimate.

11 379 + 424	**12** 981 − 477	**13** 722 + 194	**14** 626 − 398	**15** 809 − 641
16 359 + 278	**17** 1023 − 767	**18** 925 + 471	**19** 342 + 355	**20** 412 − 190

Exercise 21B

In each of the following questions:
(a) Estimate the answer by approximating the numbers to the nearest 10.
(b) Complete the calculation and compare your answer with your estimate.

1 45 + 56	**2** 62 – 34	**3** 27 + 89	**4** 132 – 66	**5** 63 + 29
6 117 + 78	**7** 174 – 38	**8** 148 – 18	**9** 81 + 47	**10** 198 – 93

In each of the following questions:
(a) Estimate the answer by approximating the numbers to the nearest 100.
(b) Complete the calculation and compare your answer with your estimate.

11 526 + 174	**12** 911 – 487	**13** 260 + 513	**14** 748 – 497	**15** 1025 – 636
16 841 + 573	**17** 1215 – 926	**18** 484 + 310	**19** 1167 – 191	**20** 845 + 116

22/ NEGATIVE NUMBERS IN CONTEXT

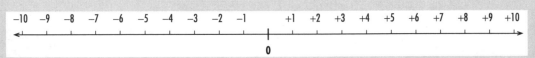

The number line above may help you to work out the answers to these questions.

> **EXAMPLE**
>
> ▶ What year is 12 years before 8 CE?
>
> > The year 8 CE can be thought of as +8.
> > So 12 years before this is –4.
> > The year is 4 BCE.
>
> (Note: CE is another way of saying AD, and BCE can be used for BC.
> For example, AD 8 = 8 CE, and 4 BC = 4 BCE.)

> **EXAMPLE**
>
> ▶ The temperature changed from –5°C to –2°C. Did the temperature rise or fall, and by how much did it change?
>
> > On the number line, –2 is to the right of –5. This means that the temperature rose.
> > The temperature rose by 3°C.

Exercise 22A

1 The temperature changed from –1°C to –4°C. Did the temperature rise or fall, and by how much did it change?

2 Tara owes the bank £211. She pays in £131. How much does she owe now?

3 What year is 20 years before 7 BC?

4 The temperature was 5°C before it dropped by 9°C. What is the new temperature?

5 A man born in 15 BCE died in 35 CE. How old was he when he died?

6 The temperature was −3°C before it rose by 3°C. What is the new temperature?

7 Susan owes £66. She repays £42. How much does she still owe?

8 The temperature changed from −8°C to −1°C. Did the temperature rise or fall, and by how much did it change?

9 My watch shows 10 minutes to 12 but my watch is 13 minutes slow. What is the real time?

10 The temperature was 4°C before it dropped by 6°C. What is the new temperature?

11 What year is 20 years after 9 BCE?

12 Ray arrives 10 minutes before his train is due to arrive. The train is 5 minutes early. How long does he have to wait?

13 John has saved £35. He needs £85. How much more does he have to save?

14 The temperature changed from −4°C to −1°C. Did the temperature rise or fall, and by how much did it change?

15 Sanjay misses his bus by 6 minutes. If the buses arrive every 20 minutes, how long does Sanjay have to wait for the next bus?

16 Shanti owes the bank £125. He pays in £150. How much money does he have in his account now?

17 The temperature was 2°C before it dropped by 12°C. What is the new temperature?

18 A train had been running 5 minutes early but stopped for 13 minutes. Is the train now early or late, and by how much?

19 The temperature changed from −7°C to −3°C. Did the temperature rise or fall, and by how much did it change?

20 What year is 8 years after 3 BCE?

Exercise 22B

1 What year is 40 years before 12 CE?

2 The temperature was −8°C before it rose by 2°C. What is the new temperature?

3 My watch is 5 minutes fast. When my watch shows 10.30, what is the correct time?

4 The temperature changed from −2°C to −11°C. Did the temperature rise or fall, and by how much did it change?

5 John owes £15. He earns £35. How much does he have left after he has paid off his debt?

6 Robin runs a race in 5 seconds under 2 minutes. Tim beat Robin by 12 seconds. What was Tim's time for the race?

7 The temperature changed from 6°C to −3°C. Did the temperature rise or fall, and by how much did it change?

8 Zakia owes £98. She repays £67. How much does she still owe?

9 The temperature was 2°C before it dropped by 5°C. What is the new temperature?

10 What year is 36 years before 4 BCE?

11 The temperature changed from −1°C to −2°C. Did the temperature rise or fall, and by how much did it change?

12 I arrive 12 minutes before a train is meant to leave but the train leaves 5 minutes early. How long do I have to wait?

13 What year is 20 years before 15 CE?

14 The temperature was 0°C before it rose by 5°C. What is the new temperature?

15 Mark owes £15. He repays £8. How much does he still owe?

16 Kishor arrives 7 minutes after his train is meant to leave but the train is 8 minutes late. How long does he have to wait?

17 The temperature changed from –7°C to –3°C. Did the temperature rise or fall, and by how much did it change?

18 Nick owes £150. He repays £85. How much does he still owe?

19 What year is 18 years after 20 BCE?

20 The temperature was –8°C before it dropped by 3°C. What is the new temperature?

23/ PROBLEMS INVOLVING MULTIPLICATION AND DIVISION WITH AND WITHOUT A CALCULATOR

Exercise 23A

Answer these questions without using a calculator.

1 What is the cost of five cards at 42p each?

2 Four tickets cost £32. How much are they each?

3 Cakes are packed into boxes in sixes. How many boxes can be filled with forty-two cakes?

4 If socks are sold in packs containing three pairs each, how many pairs are there in thirteen packs?

5 In a shop pens are sold in packets of five. How many pens are there in 24 packets?

6 How many items costing 7p each can be purchased with 84p?

7 Bill takes 12 minutes to walk a kilometre. How long would it take him to walk 5 km at this rate?

8 Six friends win £78. They share it equally. How much does each receive?

9 What is the cost of seven apples at 23p each?

10 What is the cost of six tickets at £15 each?

11 The glasses in the diagram are all the same width. What is the width of each glass?

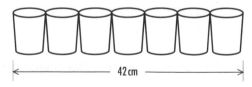

← 42 cm →

12 Potatoes are being sold in 7 kg bags. How many bags are required for 91 kg of potatoes?

13 John uses nine tiles to cover 1 square metre. How many tiles will he need for 8 square metres?

14 Spaces in a car park are 4 metres long for each car. How many spaces are there in a length of 60 metres?

15 There are six light bulbs in a pack. How many are there in 24 packs?

16 A recipe uses three times as much water as it does milk. How much water will be used with 55 ml of milk?

17 A bus passes a shop every 6 minutes. How many buses pass in an hour?

18 The height of each tin in a stack to be knocked down at the fair is 12 cm. What is the height of the stack in the diagram?

19 Stamps are sold in books of four. How many books are needed in order to have 84 stamps?

20 Sue buys crisps at 35p per bag. How much money does she need to buy eight bags?

12 cm

Exercise 23B

Answer these questions without using a calculator.

1 Six friends divide winnings of £96 equally between them. How much does each receive?

2 Adam earns £7 per hour. How much does he earn in 38 hours?

3 There are 25 sheets of paper in a pad. How many pages are there in eight pads?

4 Cans of drink cost 76p each. What is the total cost of eight cans?

5 There are six chocolate biscuits in each pack. How many packs are needed in order to have 54 biscuits?

6 Sheila can cycle 90 km each day. How far can she travel in seven days?

7 It takes Bhaveen five minutes to pack a shirt. How many shirts can he pack in an hour?

8 What is the total cost of six chocolate bars at 48p each?

9 Selma buys four pens at 75p each. What is the total cost?

10 The books in the diagram are all the same thickness. How thick is each book?

11 Troy works for eight hours a day for seven days. How many hours is this in total?

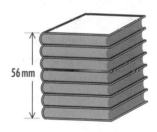

56 mm

12 There are seven apples in every 1 kg pack. How many apples will there be in 18 kg?

13 How many 5 ml doses of medicine are there in a 100 ml bottle?

14 It takes one sheet of paper to make four pages of a book. How many pages can be made from 32 sheets of paper?

15 How many sweets costing 7p each can be bought for 98p?

16 Each video tape in the diagram is 32 mm wide. How wide is the row shown?

17 Jo uses 8 cm lengths of wire to tie plants. How many lengths can he cut from 160 cm of wire?

18 Paper handkerchiefs are sold in packets of six. How many handkerchiefs are there in 18 packets?

19 There are four frozen pies in each box. How many boxes are needed for 72 pies?

20 What is the total weight of 15 parcels each weighing 9 kg?

32 mm

Exercise 23C

You may use a calculator for these questions.

1 What is the total cost of five chocolate bars at £1.25 each?

2 Donna buys four cans for £1.96. How much are they each?

3 Some tablets are sold in packs of eight. How many tablets are there in 24 packs?

4 Pens are sold in packs of six. How many packs are required for 144 pens?

5 Combs are sold on cards containing five combs. How many cards does Neil need to buy in order to have 30 combs?

6 Decoration for walls is sold in strips of length 1.5 metres. What is the total length of eight strips?

7 What is the total cost of seven photographs at 1.99 each?

8 A packet of five felt-tip pens costs 95p. How much are they each?

9 Kerry is three times as heavy as Matthew. Matthew weighs 24 kg. How much does Kerry weigh?

10 Tom is using carpet tape, which is sold in 18-metre rolls. How many rolls will Tom need in order to have 140 metres of tape?

11 How many 5 ml doses of medicine are there in a 150 ml bottle?

12 How many days are there in thirteen weeks?

13 Julie is making booklets that use eight sheets of paper. How many booklets can be made from 240 sheets of paper?

14 What is the total cost of nine chocolate bars at 27p each?

15 Some tent pegs are sold in packs of eight. Sally needs at least sixty pegs. What is the least number of packs that she should buy?

16 Apples are sold in bags of nine. How many bags do I need to buy in order to have at least 150 apples?

17 It takes a nurse 4 minutes to give an injection. How many injections can she give in 2 hours?

18 A recipe suggests 75 grams of pasta for each person. How much pasta is required for six people?

19 Yoghurts are sold in packs of twelve. How many packs are required to have at least 100 yoghurts?

20 As a special offer a supermarket gives a free can with every box of four cans. How many cans would Claire get in total if she bought twelve boxes?

Exercise 23D

You may use a calculator for these questions.

1 What is the total length of 13 panels each of length 95 cm?

2 Boxes of eggs cost £1.39 each. What is the cost of seven boxes?

3 Roger buys 5 ice creams at a total cost of £3.25. How much were they each?

4 Nickie drives 512 km in four hours on the motorway. How far is this in each hour?

5 What is the total cost of nine seat covers at £4.85 each?

6 The total bill for six light bulbs is £7.86. How much are they each?

7 There are 104 buttons on 13 cards. How many buttons are there on each card?

8 Some tropical fish are priced at £2.55 each. What is the total cost of eight fish?

9 Seven pens cost £11.20. How much are they each?

10 Nine tickets cost £135. How much are they each?

11 Fiona packs apples in bags of eight. How many bags can she fill with 248 apples?

12 What is the total cost of 5 metres of tape at £0.95 per metre?

13 How many people can be placed at nine tables each of which can seat twelve people?

14 Lawn edging is sold in 1.5-metre strips. What is the length of six strips?

15 How many 5 ml doses of medicine are there in a bottle containing 180 ml?

16 How many plastic spoons costing 8p each can be purchased with £2?

17 If I buy a pack of five chocolate wafers, I get one wafer free. How many packs do I need to buy to have 54 wafers in total?

18 Pears cost £1.15 per kilogram. What is the total cost of 7 kg?

19 Sand is eight times heavier than peat. If a bag of peat weighs 15 kg, how much will the same bag weigh when filled with sand?

20 Socks are sold in packs of three pairs. How many packs will Ruth need to buy to have at least twenty pairs of socks?

24/ PROBLEMS INVOLVING ADDITION, SUBTRACTION, MULTIPLICATION AND DIVISION WITH AND WITHOUT A CALCULATOR

Exercise 24A

Answer these questions without using a calculator.

1 Harry scores 5, 7 and 9 in his last three tests. What is his total score?

2 What is the total cost of five refills at 18p each?

3 Kath needs £5.75 but has saved only £3.50. How much more does she need?

4 Six packets of cereal cost £7.32. What is the cost of each packet?

5 In a sale the price of a hat is reduced from £9.99 to £4.49. How much is the reduction?

6 What is the total cost of eight packets of cheese biscuits at 29p each?

7 What is the length marked d in the diagram?

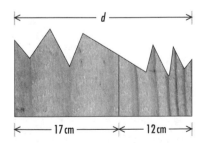

6 Fiona has 27 cassettes before she sells nine of them. How many does she have left?

9 A recipe states that each person requires 75 grams of rice. How much rice is required for six people?

10 Nine people win a total of £162. How much should they each receive?

11 Paul has saved £6.85. How much does he have after receiving £3.50 pocket money?

12 Donna cuts a hose into three equal lengths of 12 metres. What was the original length of the hose?

13 A shop reduces the cost of a pack of mackerel from £1.99 to £1.49. What is the reduction?

14 Each can in the diagram is 7 cm wide. How wide is the row of cans shown?

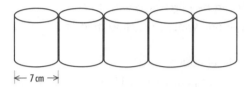

← 7 cm →

15 What is the total cost of nine articles at 65p each?

16 How many seconds are there in five minutes?

17 Some garden chairs need 62 cm of material plus an extra 17 cm for fixing. What length is required for four chairs?

18 Mary has 108 programmes from ice-hockey matches. She swaps twenty of her programmes for eight new programmes. How many does she have now?

19 What is the total cost of three adult tickets at £4 each and two children's tickets at £2.50?

20 Gill buys six plants through a mail-order catalogue. They are priced at £4 each. There is a charge for post and package of £7 on the parcel of plants. What is the total cost of the plants?

Exercise 24B

Answer these questions without using a calculator.

1 The rainfall for last year was 63 cm. This year the rainfall is 14 cm less. What is the rainfall this year?

2 Ishfaq is exactly twice the height of his little brother who is 76 cm tall. How tall is Ishfaq?

3 I spend £2.35 in one shop and £1.95 in another. How much do I spend altogether?

4 There are eight apples in each bag. How many bags are needed for 96 apples?

5 How much change do you get from £10 if you spend £6.57?

6 What is the total cost of five postcards at 24p each?

7 In a sale the price of a bag is reduced by £4 to £13. What was the original price of the bag?

8 What is the distance marked *h* in the diagram?

9 A pair of shoes costs £45 plus £6 post and packing. What is the total cost?

10 In a sale a pair of vases are reduced from £25 to £13. How much is saved on *each* vase?

11 David makes 48 sandwiches. He sells 25 of them to one shop and 18 to another. How many does he have left?

12 There are five buns in a pack. How many packs are required for 65 buns?

13 Add 36 and 43 together. Multiply the total by 6.

14 Multiply 27 by 4 and then subtract 74.

15 Some medicine is packed on cards of eight tablets. How many tablets will there be in 25 cards?

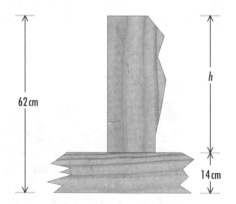

62 cm

h

14 cm

16 Four friends win £35 and £29. They share the total equally. How much does each receive?

17 Subahn's favourite crisps are normally sold in packs of twelve packets but two extra packets have been added free. Subahn decides to buy eight packs. How many packets of crisps does he have?

18 Roy saves for six weeks. He has a total of £95 but started with £47. How much did he save per week?

19 A theatre company sells 82 tickets in advance and another 42 on the night. Twenty-four people who had bought tickets did not turn up. How many people were in the audience?

20 A man reached the age of 63 in 1972. In which year was he born?

Exercise 24C

You may use a calculator to answer these questions.

1 A theatre has an audience of 145 on Friday and 196 on Saturday. What was the total for the two days?

2 A store has 176 boxes of tissues. Of these 78 boxes are sold. How many remain?

3 Cat food is packed in boxes each of which contains 24 tins. How many tins are there in seven boxes?

4 How many minutes playing time is there on four tapes if each tape lasts 180 minutes?

5 If 400 grams of spaghetti is shared between five people, how much does each receive?

6 Ruth scores 95 and 89 in two tests. What is her total mark?

7 The boxes in the diagram are all the same width. What is the width of each box?

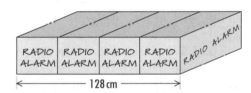

8 At a rugby game there are 155 people in seats and 237 people standing. How many people are there in total?

9 How many seconds are there in 1 minute 45 seconds?

10 Six boxes contain a total of 240 tin openers. How many are there in each box?

11 Some cassettes last 90 minutes. How long do five cassettes last?

12 The diagram shows a stack of plywood. What is the thickness of each sheet?

13 Paul has a bag of flour containing 425 gram and another containing 350 gram. What is the total weight?

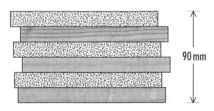

14 Wendy opens a bottle containing 520 ml of a chemical. She uses 345 ml. How much is left?

15 There are 275 ml remaining in a bottle after 350 ml have been used. How much was in the bottle originally?

16 A can of drink normally contains 440 ml but has extra added as a special offer so that it now contains 500 ml. How much extra is there in eight cans?

17 There are 15 extra snack bars in every bag that normally holds 36. How many bars are there in total in seven bags?

18 How many plates are there in total in five boxes of eight plates and seven boxes of six plates?

19 The normal price for a cake is £1.99 but it has been reduced to £1.45. What is the saving on five such cakes?

20 Some eggs are packed in boxes of twenty-four but the machine that packs the eggs has a fault and breaks five eggs in every box. How many unbroken eggs are there in eight boxes?

Exercise 24D

You may use a calculator to answer these questions.

1 Each carton in the diagram is 9 cm wide. How wide is the shelf?

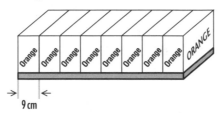

9 cm

2 There are 109 people at a dinner but only 71 of them stay on to the disco afterwards. How many people leave?

3 The attendances for five classes are 28, 26, 30, 25 and 29. What is the total attendance?

4 Seven packs of ice cream cost a total of £9.10. What is the cost of each pack?

5 In a sale the price of a coat is reduced form £76 to £38. By how much has the price been reduced?

6 One bottle of shampoo contains 125 ml. How much do eight bottles contain?

7 The boxes in the diagram are all the same height. What is the height of each box?

8 Graham buys a radio through the post. The price is £45.95 but there is a charge of £6.95 post and packing. What is the total cost of the radio?

9 A packet of a chocolate drink contains 225 grams. What is the weight of eight packets?

10 Rhiannon opens a 500-gram pack of rice. She uses 325 grams. How much rice remains?

11 The cost of nine tickets is £135. What is the price of each ticket?

12 What is the total cost of six chocolate bars at 46p each?

13 At a hockey game there are 354 people sitting and 465 standing. How many people are there in total?

14 A video recorder priced at £299 is reduced by £75. What is the price now?

15 The three angles of a triangle add up to 180°. If one angle is 45° and another is 87°, what is the size of the third angle?

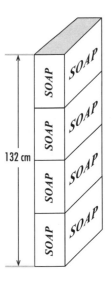

132 cm

16 Multiply 21 by 5 and then divide by 7.

17 Divide 72 by 4 and then multiply by 6.

18 The normal price of a bottle of sauce is £1.95 but it is reduced to £1.49. How much does Colin save in total if he buys three bottles?

19 Fiona buys six packs each containing eight paper cups. She buys five packs each containing six cups. How many cups does she have altogether?

20 Suhara can buy postcards priced at 25p or 32p. What is the total difference in price if she buys 20 cards?

25/ RECOGNISING SIMPLE FRACTIONS

EXAMPLE

► What fraction is shaded in the diagram?

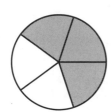

The shape is divided into five equal portions:
each is $\frac{1}{5}$.

There are three of these portions
and so the shaded area is $\frac{3}{5}$.

Exercise 25A

There are 20 numbered, shaded areas. State what fraction each area is of the whole shape.

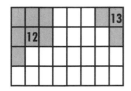 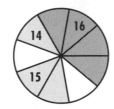 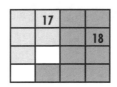 

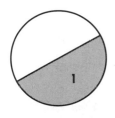 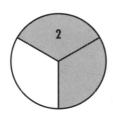 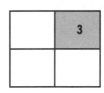 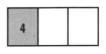

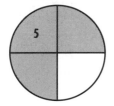 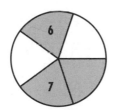 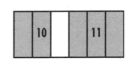 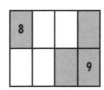

Exercise 25B

There are 20 numbered, shaded areas. State what fraction each is of the whole shape.

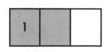   

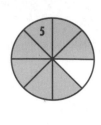
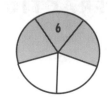

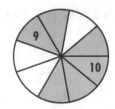

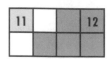
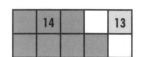

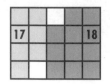

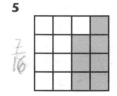

Exercise 25C

State the fraction of the diagram that is shaded and also the fraction that is *not* shaded.

1
$\frac{1}{4}$

2
$\frac{1}{3}$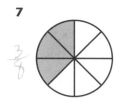

3
$\frac{1}{8}$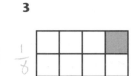

4
$\frac{2}{5}$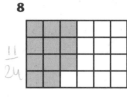

5
$\frac{7}{16}$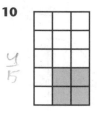

6
$\frac{2}{9}$

7
$\frac{3}{8}$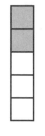

8
$\frac{11}{24}$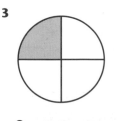

9
$\frac{3}{8}$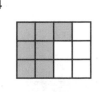

10
$\frac{4}{5}$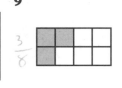

Exercise 25D

State the fraction of the diagram that is shaded and also the fraction that is *not* shaded.

1

2

3

4

5

6

7

8

9
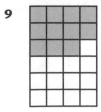

10
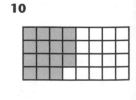

26/ DRAWING SIMPLE FRACTIONS

EXAMPLE

▶ Draw a diagram to show $\frac{3}{4}$ of a circle.

EXAMPLE

▶ Draw a diagram to show $\frac{5}{8}$ of a rectangle.

Exercise 26A

Draw a diagram to show each of the following fractions. Use the shape indicated in the brackets.

1 $\frac{2}{3}$ (circle)　　　**2** $\frac{1}{4}$ (circle)　　　**3** $\frac{1}{2}$ (rectangle)　　　**4** $\frac{3}{5}$ (rectangle)

5 $\frac{1}{8}$ (rectangle)　　　**6** $\frac{3}{8}$ (square)　　　**7** $\frac{3}{4}$ (square)　　　**8** $\frac{1}{3}$ (circle)

9 $\frac{2}{5}$ (circle)　　　**10** $\frac{5}{12}$ (rectangle)　　　**11** $\frac{2}{9}$ and $\frac{4}{9}$ on the same diagram (square)

12 $\frac{1}{5}$ and $\frac{4}{5}$ on the same diagram (circle)　　　**13** $\frac{7}{15}$ and $\frac{4}{15}$ on the same diagram (rectangle)

14 $\frac{3}{20}$ and $\frac{11}{20}$ on the same diagram (rectangle)　　　**15** $\frac{1}{25}$ and $\frac{14}{25}$ on the same diagram (rectangle)

Exercise 26B

Draw a diagram to show each of the following fractions. Use the shape indicated in the brackets.

1 $\frac{1}{3}$ (rectangle)　　　**2** $\frac{3}{16}$ (rectangle)　　　**3** $\frac{7}{10}$ (rectangle)　　　**4** $\frac{4}{5}$ (circle)

5 $\frac{1}{2}$ (circle)　　　**6** $\frac{3}{8}$ (rectangle)　　　**7** $\frac{2}{5}$ (rectangle)　　　**8** $\frac{1}{8}$ (circle)

9 $\frac{5}{9}$ (square)　　　**10** $\frac{7}{12}$ (rectangle)　　　**11** $\frac{5}{16}$ and $\frac{4}{16}$ on the same diagram (square)

12 $\frac{1}{10}$ and $\frac{7}{10}$ on the same diagram (rectangle)　　　**13** $\frac{1}{5}$ and $\frac{2}{5}$ on the same diagram (circle)

14 $\frac{11}{24}$ and $\frac{7}{24}$ on the same diagram (rectangle)　　　**15** $\frac{5}{12}$ and $\frac{7}{12}$ on the same diagram (rectangle)

27/ FRACTIONS OF QUANTITIES

EXAMPLE

▶ Find $\frac{1}{4}$ of 96.

$\frac{1}{4}$ of 96 = 96 ÷ 4

= 24

EXAMPLE

▶ Find $\frac{1}{10}$ of £4.50.

$\frac{1}{10}$ of £4.50 = £4.50 ÷ 10

= £0.45

Exercise 27A

Work out the following.

1. $\frac{1}{8}$ of 40   40÷8=5

2. $\frac{1}{2}$ of 56 kg

3. $\frac{1}{10}$ of £20

4. $\frac{1}{3}$ of 36 cm

5. $\frac{1}{9}$ of 45 km

6. $\frac{1}{2}$ of £24

7. $\frac{1}{8}$ of £48

8. $\frac{1}{3}$ of 27 kg

9. $\frac{1}{4}$ of £32

10. $\frac{1}{2}$ of £110

11. $\frac{1}{3}$ of 18 hours

12. $\frac{1}{6}$ of £42

13. $\frac{1}{5}$ of £40

14. $\frac{1}{10}$ of £5

15. $\frac{1}{4}$ of 48

16. $\frac{1}{7}$ of 105 ml

17. $\frac{1}{6}$ of 72

18. $\frac{1}{15}$ of 30 minutes

19. $\frac{1}{5}$ of 25 g

20. $\frac{1}{4}$ of 100

Exercise 27B

Work out the following.

1. $\frac{1}{5}$ of £10

2. $\frac{1}{3}$ of £60

3. $\frac{1}{2}$ of £4.50

4. $\frac{1}{4}$ of 80 km

5. $\frac{1}{8}$ of 16 km

6. $\frac{1}{3}$ of 48 hours

7. $\frac{1}{6}$ of £12

8. $\frac{1}{8}$ of 32p

9. $\frac{1}{4}$ of 64 km

10. $\frac{1}{2}$ of 38 ml

11. $\frac{1}{10}$ of 200 m

12. $\frac{1}{6}$ of 42 minutes

13. $\frac{1}{7}$ of £14

14. $\frac{1}{2}$ of £5

15. $\frac{1}{8}$ of £32

16. $\frac{1}{7}$ of 35

17. $\frac{1}{10}$ of £40

18. $\frac{1}{5}$ of £4

19. $\frac{1}{6}$ of 54 minutes

20. $\frac{1}{18}$ of 36 m

28/ RECOGNISING AND DRAWING SIMPLE PERCENTAGES

$1\% = \dfrac{1}{100}$

EXAMPLE

► What percentage of the diagram is shaded as A and as B?

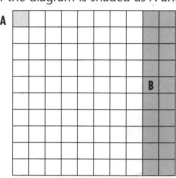

There are 100 squares in the diagram. This means that each one is $\dfrac{1}{100}$ (or 1%) of the whole.

A is 1 square so is 1%.
B is 20 squares and is 20%.

Exercise 28A

For each labelled area state the percentage of the diagram that is shaded.

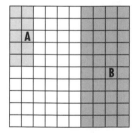
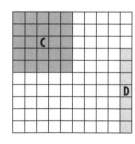
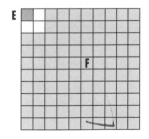
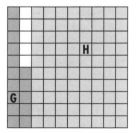

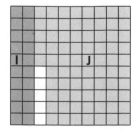
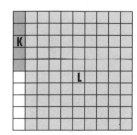
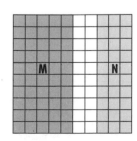
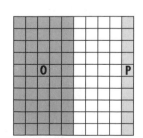

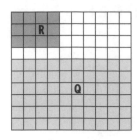
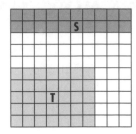

Exercise 28B

For each labelled area state the percentage of the diagram that is shaded.

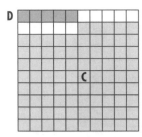
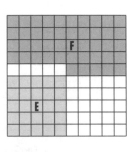
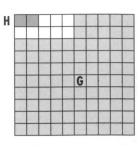

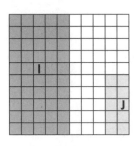
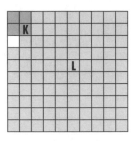
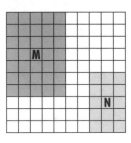
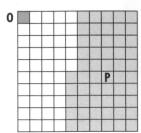

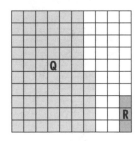
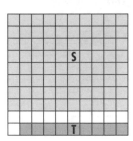

Exercise 28C

For each question draw a grid with 100 squares. Shade and label the following percentages.

1	50% and 20%	**2**	25% and 30%	**3**	65% and 10%	**4**	5% and 75%
5	10% and 60%	**6**	1% and 35%	**7**	90% and 3%	**8**	40% and 45%
9	80% and 15%	**10**	15% and 70%	**11**	30% and 70%	**12**	75% and 10%
13	40% and 15%	**14**	85% and 5%	**15**	25% and 60%	**16**	55% and 20%
17	2% and 95%	**18**	90% and 10%	**19**	35% and 45%	**20**	80% and 7%

Exercise 28D

For each question draw a grid with 100 squares. Shade and label the following percentages.

1	90% and 1%	**2**	20% and 75%	**3**	80% and 5%	**4**	85% and 12%
5	25% and 60%	**6**	40% and 50%	**7**	95% and 5%	**8**	55% and 45%
9	35% and 65%	**10**	70% and 30%	**11**	83% and 16%	**12**	15% and 75%
13	50% and 30%	**14**	60% and 32%	**15**	42% and 48%	**16**	1% and 99%
17	37% and 61%	**18**	85% and 5%	**19**	19% and 81%	**20**	69% and 31%

29/ CONVERSION BETWEEN SIMPLE FRACTIONS AND PERCENTAGES

Remember that 1% means $\frac{1}{100}$ and so 7% = $\frac{7}{100}$, 13% = $\frac{13}{100}$.

There are some simple conversions which are worth remembering:

1% = $\frac{1}{100}$	15% = $\frac{3}{20}$	40% = $\frac{2}{5}$	65% = $\frac{13}{20}$	90% = $\frac{9}{10}$
2% = $\frac{1}{50}$	20% = $\frac{1}{5}$	45% = $\frac{9}{20}$	70% = $\frac{7}{10}$	95% = $\frac{19}{20}$
4% = $\frac{1}{25}$	25% = $\frac{1}{4}$	50% = $\frac{1}{2}$	75% = $\frac{1}{5}$	100% = 1
5% = $\frac{1}{20}$	30% = $\frac{3}{10}$	55% = $\frac{11}{20}$	80% = $\frac{4}{5}$	$33\frac{1}{3}$% = $\frac{1}{3}$
10% = $\frac{1}{10}$	35% = $\frac{7}{20}$	60% = $\frac{3}{5}$	85% = $\frac{17}{20}$	$66\frac{2}{3}$% = $\frac{2}{3}$

Exercise 29A

Convert to percentages.

1	$\frac{1}{4}$	**2**	$\frac{3}{4}$	**3**	$\frac{1}{5}$	**4**	$\frac{9}{10}$	**5**	$\frac{2}{5}$
6	$\frac{1}{100}$	**7**	$\frac{1}{2}$	**8**	$\frac{3}{10}$	**9**	$\frac{4}{5}$	**10**	$\frac{97}{100}$
11	$\frac{1}{3}$	**12**	$\frac{1}{10}$	**13**	$\frac{7}{10}$	**14**	$\frac{3}{5}$	**15**	$\frac{1}{20}$
16	$\frac{83}{100}$	**17**	$\frac{7}{10}$	**18**	$\frac{29}{100}$	**19**	$\frac{17}{100}$	**20**	$\frac{2}{3}$

Exercise 29B

Convert to percentages.

1 $\frac{3}{5}$		**2** $\frac{2}{3}$		**3** $\frac{1}{5}$		**4** $\frac{1}{2}$		**5** $\frac{7}{20}$
6 $\frac{1}{10}$		**7** $\frac{9}{10}$		**8** $\frac{3}{4}$		**9** $\frac{1}{100}$		**10** $\frac{1}{4}$
11 $\frac{4}{5}$		**12** $\frac{3}{20}$		**13** $\frac{11}{20}$		**14** $\frac{1}{20}$		**15** $\frac{73}{100}$
16 $\frac{1}{3}$		**17** $\frac{1}{25}$		**18** $\frac{19}{20}$		**19** $\frac{1}{50}$		**20** $\frac{83}{100}$

Exercise 29C

Convert to fractions.

1 20%		**2** 25%		**3** 30%		**4** 4%		**5** 60%
6 40%		**7** 65%		**8** 80%		**9** 2%		**10** $33\frac{1}{3}$%
11 50%		**12** 5%		**13** 61%		**14** 10%		**15** 75%
16 1%		**17** 15%		**18** 99%		**19** 70%		**20** 11%

Exercise 29D

Convert to fractions.

1 80%		**2** 5%		**3** 30%		**4** 70%		**5** 40%
6 50%		**7** 77%		**8** 75%		**9** 45%		**10** 9%
11 20%		**12** $33\frac{1}{3}$%		**13** 6%		**14** 19%		**15** 25%
16 10%		**17** 85%		**18** 55%		**19** 3%		**20** $66\frac{2}{3}$%

30./ SIMPLE PERCENTAGES OF SUMS OF MONEY

1% of £1 is 1p.

EXAMPLE
▶ Find 5% of £2.

5% of £2 = 5p × 2
= 10p

EXAMPLE
▶ Find 8% of £20.

8% of £20 = 8p × 20
= 160p
= £1.60

Exercise 30A

1 3% of £4	**2** 2% of £5	**3** 5% of £1	**4** 4% of £7
5 7% of £1	**6** 3% of £2	**7** 4% of £6	**8** 8% of £6
9 1% of £8	**10** 5% of £4	**11** 9% of £3	**12** 8% of £1
13 13% of £1	**14** 6% of £2	**15** 9% of £1	**16** 3% of £6
17 2% of £7	**18** 4% of £4	**19** 1% of £45	**20** 3% of £5
21 6% of £6	**22** 4% of £8	**23** 6% of £3	**24** 1% of £13
25 7% of £2	**26** 5% of £9	**27** 3% of £3	**28** 9% of £5
29 8% of £3	**30** 7% of £4	**31** 10% of £2	**32** 8% of £8
33 1% of £17	**34** 10% of £5	**35** 4% of £9	**36** 5% of £6
37 2% of £6	**38** 6% of £5	**39** 4% of £5	**40** 7% of £11

Exercise 30B

1 5% of £3	**2** 3% of £5	**3** 5% of £7	**4** 10% of £3
5 3% of £11	**6** 8% of £2	**7** 6% of £4	**8** 2% of £13
9 4% of £2	**10** 1% of £13	**11** 14% of £2	**12** 6% of £7
13 4% of £3	**14** 9% of £2	**15** 7% of £5	**16** 3% of £9
17 12% of £3	**18** 10% of £7	**19** 9% of £6	**20** 5% of £8
21 85% of £1	**22** 8% of £4	**23** 5% of £11	**24** 2% £12
25 3% of £8	**26** 6% of £5	**27** 2% of £16	**28** 3% of £6
29 8% of £5	**30** 4% 0f £10	**31** 7% of £6	**32** 4% of £11
33 10% of £4	**34** 9% of £7	**35** 17% of £1	**36** 7% of £8
37 15% of £2	**38** 10% of £13	**39** 4% of £7	**40** 1% of £94

REVISION

Exercise B

Work out the following without using a calculator.

1 Give answers to these division questions to the nearest whole number.
(a) 36 ÷ 5 **7**   (b) 23 ÷ 6 **19**   (c) 21 ÷ 4 **5**   (d) 40 ÷ 7 **6**

2 Approximate the following (i) to the nearest 10 (ii) to the nearest 100.
(a) 174 **170 200**   (b) 216 **220 200** (c) 888 **890 900**   (d) 1049 **1050 1000**

3 (i) Estimate the answer to the following calculations and (ii) complete the calculation in order to see if your estimate was good.
(a) 58 + 63 **120** (b) 129 − 72 **60** (c) 97 + 84 **180** (d) 142 − 37 **100**

4 What year is 12 years before 3 CE?

9 BCE

5 What fraction of each of these diagrams is shaded?

(a) 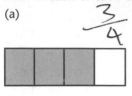 $\frac{3}{4}$

(b) 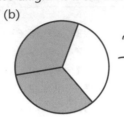 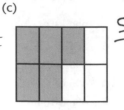 $\frac{2}{3}$

(c) $\frac{5}{8}$

(d) 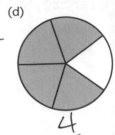 $\frac{4}{5}$

6 Shade the fraction stated using the shape indicated.

(a) $\frac{2}{3}$ (circle) (b) $\frac{7}{8}$ (rectangle) (c) $\frac{5}{9}$ (square) (d) $\frac{2}{5}$ (circle)

7 Calculate: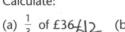

(a) $\frac{1}{3}$ of £36 £12 (b) $\frac{1}{4}$ of 24 kg 6 kg (c) $\frac{1}{8}$ of 16 ml 2 ml (d) $\frac{1}{10}$ of £120 £12

8 For each labelled area state the percentage of the diagram that is shaded.

(a)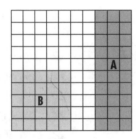

(b)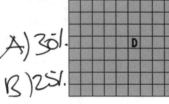

A) 30%.

B) 25%.

D) 85%

C) 7%

9 Convert to percentages:

(a) $\frac{3}{4}$ 75%. (b) $\frac{1}{2}$ 50%. (b) $\frac{1}{5}$ 20%. (d) $\frac{1}{4}$ 25%.

10 Convert to fractions:

(a) 20% $\frac{1}{5}$ (b) 10% $\frac{1}{10}$ (c) 5% $\frac{1}{20}$ (d) 75% $\frac{3}{4}$

11 Calculate:

(a) 4% of £2 8p (b) 7% of £3 21p (c) 5% of £4 20p (d) 8% of £50 £4

Exercise BB

1 Joy is cutting strips of card 6 cm wide. How many strips can she cut from a piece of card that is 50 cm wide and how wide is the piece that is left?

2 Paul is running at a steady speed and covers 1 km every 7 minutes. How many kilometres will he cover in an hour to the nearest kilometre.

3 The crowd at a sporting event is reported as being 5135. How many is this to the nearest 100?

4 If 245 people go to the local theatre, how many is this to the nearest ten?

5 Tim spends £1.23, £2.29 and 98p on items in a supermarket. He has a £5 note. Without working out how much he has to pay exactly, estimate whether Tim has enough money. Now work it out exactly.

6 The temperature changes from −3°C to −5°C. Has it become warmer or colder, and by how much has the temperature changed?

7 Clare needs £3 but has saved only £2.45. How much more does she need?

8   What is the total cost of five pencils at 17p each?

9   The normal price of a cake is £2.99 but it is reduced to £2.49. How much do you save on each cake? Camilla buys three; how much does she save altogether?

10   The total cost of three packets of nuts is 96p. What is the cost of each packet?

11   If 137 tickets are sold in advance and 95 are sold on the day, how many tickets are sold altogether?

12   How much of the cake shown has been eaten and how much remains?

13   How much of the rectangle shown is shaded and how much is *not* shaded?

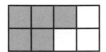

14   Draw a rectangle and shade $\frac{3}{10}$ of it.

15   Draw a circle and shade $\frac{1}{3}$ of it.

16   Pieter uses $\frac{1}{5}$ of a jar containing 400 grams of jam. How many grams remain?

17   The safety limit on a lift is 12 tonnes. It is loaded to $\frac{3}{4}$ of this amount. What is the weight of the load?

18   Copy the 10 × 10 grid shown and shade 30% (label this A) and 45% (label this B). What percentage of the grid remains unshaded?

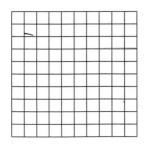

19   In a sale everything is reduced by 25%. What fraction is this?

20   I estimate that I have done $\frac{1}{5}$ of my work. What percentage is this?

21   Prices have been reduced by 10%. What is the saving on a pack of batteries originally priced at £5?

22   Una has saved 30% of £6. How much has she saved?

Algebra

31/ NUMBER PATTERNS

EXAMPLE
▶ State the next two terms in this number pattern: 7, 9, 11, 13, ..., ...

The next two numbers are 15 and 17.

EXAMPLE
▶ State the next two terms of this number pattern and say what the pattern is:
4, 7, 10, 13, ..., ...

The next two numbers are 16 and 19 because each term is 3 more than the previous term.

EXAMPLE
▶ State the next two terms in this number pattern and say what the pattern is:
12, 15, 18, 21, ..., ...

The next two numbers are 24 and 27; these are multiples of 3 greater than 10.

EXAMPLE
▶ State the next two terms of this number pattern and say what the pattern is:
2, 3, 5, 8, ..., ...

The next two numbers are 12 and 17 because the difference between each term is increasing by one.

Exercise 31A

State the next two terms in each number pattern.

1 2, 4, 6, 8, ..., ...

2 5, 7, 9, 11, ..., ...

3 5, 6, 7, 8, ..., ...

4 3, 6, 9, 12, ..., ...

5 65, 60, 55, 50, ..., ...

6 9, 11, 13, 15, ..., ...

7 13, 12, 11, 10, ..., ...

8 5, 10, 15, 20, ..., ...

9 7, 14, 21, 28, ..., ...

10 1, 4, 7, 10, ..., ...

11 7, 11, 15, 19, ..., ...

12 25, 27, 29, 31, ..., ...

13 50, 45, 40, 35, ..., ...

14 11, 21, 31, 41, ..., ...

15 11, 14, 17, 20, ..., ...

16 30, 28, 26, 24, ..., ...   **17** 40, 20, 10, ..., ...   **18** 32, 34, 36, 38, ..., ...
19 1, 2, 4, 8, ..., ...   **20** 5, 10, 20, 40, ..., ...

Exercise 31B

State the next two terms in each number pattern.

1 7, 9, 11, 13, ..., ...   **2** 6, 9, 12, 15 ..., ...   **3** 14, 24, 34, 44, ..., ...
4 30, 27, 24, 21, ..., ...   **5** 8, 10, 12, 14, ..., ...   **6** 12, 17, 22, 27, ..., ...
7 40, 37, 34, 31, ..., ...   **8** 21, 28, 35, 42, ..., ...   **9** 18, 16, 14, 12, ..., ...
10 50, 43, 36, 29, ..., ...   **11** 24, 21, 18, 15, ..., ...   **12** 56, 51, 46, 41, ..., ...
13 8, 12, 16, 20, ..., ...   **14** 10, 16, 22, 28, ..., ...   **15** 25, 20, 15, 10, ..., ...
16 72, 63, 54, 45, ..., ...   **17** 25, 50, 75, 100, ..., ...   **18** 2, 3, 5, 8, ..., ...
19 64, 32, 16, 8, ..., ...   **20** 8, 6, 4, 2, ..., ...

Exercise 31C

State the next two terms in each number pattern and say what the pattern is.

1 2, 4, 6, 8, ..., ...   **2** 12, 11, 10, 9, ..., ...   **3** 33, 31, 29, 27, ..., ...
4 2, 4, 8, 16, ..., ...   **5** 6, 8, 10, 12, ..., ...   **6** 26, 22, 18, 14, ..., ...
7 9, 12, 15, 18, ..., ...   **8** 15, 18, 21, 24, ..., ...   **9** 65, 67, 69, 71, ..., ...
10 23, 25, 27, 29, ..., ...   **11** 4, 10, 16, 22, ..., ...   **12** 55, 44, 33, 22, ..., ...
13 1, 10, 19, 28, ..., ...   **14** 35, 34, 32, 29, ..., ...   **15** 200, 100, 50, 25, ..., ...
16 65, 55, 45, 35, ..., ...   **17** 90, 82, 74, 66, ..., ...   **18** 1, 3, 6, 10, ..., ...
19 2, $2\frac{1}{2}$, 3, $3\frac{1}{2}$, ..., ...   **20** 8, 4, 2 , 1, ..., ...

Exercise 31D

State the next two terms in each number pattern and say what the pattern is.

1 1, 3, 5, 7, ..., ...   **2** 17, 15, 13, 11, ..., ...   **3** 15, 14, 13, 12, ..., ...
4 11, 14, 17, 20, ..., ...   **5** 34, 30, 26, 22, ..., ...   **6** 18, 27, 36, 45, ..., ...
7 12, 14, 16, 18, ..., ...   **8** 8, 11, 14, 17, ..., ...   **9** 4, 8, 12, 16, ..., ...
10 36, 33, 30, 27, ..., ...   **11** 5, 13, 21, 29, ..., ...   **12** 32, 31, 30, 29, ..., ...
13 5, 7, 9, 11, ..., ...   **14** 144, 72, 36, 18, ..., ...   **15** 10, 13, 17, 22, ..., ...
16 50, 49, 47, 44, ..., ...   **17** 6, 8, 11, 15, ..., ...   **18** 1, 4, 9, 16, ..., ...
19 85, 80, 75, 70, ..., ...   **20** 10, 7, 4, 1, ..., ...

32/ FUNCTION MACHINES: FINDING OUTPUTS

A **function machine** acts on an **input** and changes it. The new number is called the **output**.

5 (input) $\rightarrow$ $\boxed{\times 2}$ $\rightarrow$ $\boxed{+3}$ $\rightarrow$ **13** (output)

The function machine above multiplies the input by 2 and then adds 3.

EXAMPLE

▶ in $\rightarrow$ $\boxed{\times 3}$ $\rightarrow$ $\boxed{+2}$ $\rightarrow$ out

State the outputs from the function machine for these inputs:

(a) 3   (b) 5   (c) 7   (d) 9

Outputs:

(a) $3 \rightarrow \boxed{\times 3} \rightarrow 9 \rightarrow \boxed{+2} \rightarrow 11$ (b) $5 \rightarrow \boxed{\times 3} \rightarrow 15 \rightarrow \boxed{+2} \rightarrow 17$

(c) $7 \rightarrow \boxed{\times 3} \rightarrow 21 \rightarrow \boxed{+2} \rightarrow 23$ (d) $9 \rightarrow \boxed{\times 3} \rightarrow 27 \rightarrow \boxed{+2} \rightarrow 29$

Exercise 32A

For each of the function machines, state the *outputs* for the given inputs.

1   in $\rightarrow$ $\boxed{\times 2}$ $\rightarrow$ $\boxed{+1}$ $\rightarrow$ out
(a) 2   (b) 4   (c) 6   (d) 8

2   in $\rightarrow$ $\boxed{\times 3}$ $\rightarrow$ $\boxed{+5}$ $\rightarrow$ out
(a) 0   (b) 3   (c) 6   (d) 9

3   in $\rightarrow$ $\boxed{\times 2}$ $\rightarrow$ $\boxed{-1}$ $\rightarrow$ out
(a) 1   (b) 3   (c) 5   (d) 7

4   in $\rightarrow$ $\boxed{\times 5}$ $\rightarrow$ $\boxed{+3}$ $\rightarrow$ out
(a) 1   (b) 2   (c) 3   (d) 4

5   in $\rightarrow$ $\boxed{\times 3}$ $\rightarrow$ $\boxed{-2}$ $\rightarrow$ out
(a) 2   (b) 4   (c) 6   (d) 8

6   in $\rightarrow$ $\boxed{\times 2}$ $\rightarrow$ $\boxed{-5}$ $\rightarrow$ out
(a) 6   (b) 7   (c) 8   (d) 9

7   in $\rightarrow$ $\boxed{\times 5}$ $\rightarrow$ $\boxed{+2}$ $\rightarrow$ out
(a) 0   (b) 1   (c) 2   (d) 3

8   in $\rightarrow$ $\boxed{\times 3}$ $\rightarrow$ $\boxed{-4}$ $\rightarrow$ out
(a) 10   (b) 8   (c) 6   (d) 2

9   in $\rightarrow$ $\boxed{\times 4}$ $\rightarrow$ $\boxed{+5}$ $\rightarrow$ out
(a) 2   (b) 4   (c) 6   (d) 8

10   in $\rightarrow$ $\boxed{\times \frac{1}{2}}$ $\rightarrow$ $\boxed{-1}$ $\rightarrow$ out
(a) 2   (b) 4   (c) 6   (d) 8

Exercise 32B

For each of the function machines, state the *outputs* for the given inputs:

1   in $\rightarrow$ $\boxed{\times 4}$ $\rightarrow$ $\boxed{+2}$ $\rightarrow$ out
(a) 1   (b) 3   (c) 5   (d) 7

2   in $\rightarrow$ $\boxed{\times 2}$ $\rightarrow$ $\boxed{-3}$ $\rightarrow$ out
(a) 4   (b) 6   (c) 8   (d) 10

3   in $\rightarrow$ $\boxed{\times 5}$ $\rightarrow$ $\boxed{-1}$ $\rightarrow$ out
(a) 2   (b) 4   (c) 6   (d) 8

4   in $\rightarrow$ $\boxed{\times 3}$ $\rightarrow$ $\boxed{+1}$ $\rightarrow$ out
(a) 11   (b) 9   (c) 7   (d) 5

5   in $\rightarrow$ $\boxed{\times 2}$ $\rightarrow$ $\boxed{+5}$ $\rightarrow$ out
(a) 1   (b) 3   (c) 5   (d) 9

6   in $\rightarrow$ $\boxed{\times 3}$ $\rightarrow$ $\boxed{-3}$ $\rightarrow$ out
(a) 10   (b) 20   (c) 30   (d) 40

7   in $\rightarrow$ $\boxed{\times 6}$ $\rightarrow$ $\boxed{+1}$ $\rightarrow$ out
(a) 0   (b) 2   (c) 4   (d) 6

8   in $\rightarrow$ $\boxed{\times 2}$ $\rightarrow$ $\boxed{+3}$ $\rightarrow$ out
(a) 5   (b) 10   (c) 15   (d) 20

9   in $\rightarrow$ $\boxed{\times 4}$ $\rightarrow$ $\boxed{-2}$ $\rightarrow$ out
(a) 5   (b) 4   (c) 3   (d) 2

10   in $\rightarrow$ $\boxed{\times \frac{1}{2}}$ $\rightarrow$ $\boxed{-5}$ $\rightarrow$ out
(a) 20   (b) 16   (c) 12   (d) 8

33/ FUNCTION MACHINES: FINDING THE FUNCTION

In these exercises the inputs and outputs are given; you have to find out what function is needed in the function machine.

> **EXAMPLE**
>
> ▶ Find the function needed to give these outputs from the inputs.
>
> 1, 2, 3, 4 → ? → 3, 4, 5, 6
>
> The function is '+ 2'.

> **EXAMPLE**
>
> ▶ Find the function needed to give these outputs from the inputs.
>
> 2, 3, 4, 5 → ? → 4, 6, 8, 10
>
> The function is '× 2'.

Exercise 33A

State the function required to give these outputs from the inputs.

1 4, 3, 2, 1 → ? → 5, 4, 3, 2
2 2, 4, 6, 8 → ? → 1, 3, 5, 7
3 1, 3, 5, 7 → ? → 7, 9, 11, 13
4 3, 2, 1, 0 → ? → 6, 4, 2, 0
5 0, 2, 4, 6 → ? → 0, 6, 12, 18
6 1, 2, 3, 4 → ? → 0,1, 2, 3
7 8, 6, 4, 2 → ? → 6, 4, 2, 0
8 2, 4, 6, 8 → ? → 3, 5, 7, 9
9 2, 6,10, 14 → ? → 6, 10, 14, 18
10 0, 5, 10, 15 → ? → 0, 10, 20, 30
11 1, 2, 3, 4 → ? → 4, 8, 12, 16
12 8, 6, 4, 2 → ? → 10, 8, 6, 4
13 0, 1, 2, 3 → ? → 6, 7, 8, 9
14 7, 6, 5, 4 → ? → 4, 3, 2, 1
15 2, 4, 6, 8 → ? → 14, 28, 42, 56
16 7, 5, 3, 1 → ? → 70, 50, 30, 10
17 3, 6, 9, 12 → ? → 0, 3, 6, 9
18 4, 5, 6, 7 → ? → 6, 7, 8, 9
19 2, 3, 4, 5 → ? → 5, 6, 7, 8
20 4, 3, 2, 1 → ? → 3, 2, 1, 0
21 1, 3, 5, 7 → ? → 2, 6, 10, 14
22 6, 4, 2, 0 → ? → 11, 9, 7, 5
23 0, 5, 10, 15 → ? → 0, 15, 30, 45
24 6, 4, 2, 0 → ? → 9, 7, 5, 3
25 8, 6, 4, 2 → ? → 4, 3, 2, 1
26 3, 2, 1, 0 → ? → 13, 12, 11, 10
27 4, 6, 8, 10 → ? → 2, 4, 6, 8
28 8, 10, 12, 14 → ? → 2, 4, 6, 8
29 2, 6, 10, 14 → ? → 1, 3, 5, 7
30 1, 2, 3, 4 → ? → 6, 12, 18, 24

Exercise 33B

State the function required to give these outputs from the inputs.

1 1, 2, 3, 4 → ? → 8, 16, 24, 32
2 2, 4, 6, 8 → ? → 6, 8, 10, 12
3 1, 3, 5, 7 → ? → 3, 9, 15, 21
4 7, 5, 3, 1 → ? → 11, 9, 7, 5

5 9, 8, 7, 6 → ? → 5, 4, 3, 2

6 0, 2, 4, 6 → ? → 0, 2, 4, 6

7 4, 3, 2, 1 → ? → 36, 27, 18, 9

8 0, 2, 4, 6 → ? → 0, 20, 40, 60

9 4, 5, 6, 7 → ? → 0, 1, 2, 3

10 6, 7, 8, 9 → ? → 11, 12, 13, 14

11 1, 3, 5, 7 → ? → 0, 2, 4, 6

12 10, 12, 14, 16 → ? → 5, 6, 7, 8

13 7, 5, 3, 1 → ? → 9, 7, 5, 3

14 1, 2, 3, 4 → ? → 4, 8, 12, 16

15 8, 6, 4, 2 → ? → 6, 4, 2, 0

16 1, 3, 5, 7 → ? → 2, 4, 6, 8

17 7, 6, 5, 4 → ? → 6, 5, 4, 3

18 4, 3, 2, 1 → ? → 12, 9, 6, 3

19 2, 4, 6, 8 → ? → 8, 16, 24, 32

20 3, 2, 1, 0 → ? → 21, 14, 7, 0

21 0, 1, 2, 3 → ? → 0, 5, 10, 15

22 8, 6, 4, 2 → ? → 11, 9, 7, 5

23 15, 10, 5, 0 → ? → 3, 2, 1, 0

24 9, 8, 7, 6 → ? → 3, 2, 1, 0

25 4, 3, 2, 1 → ? → 20, 15, 10, 5

26 15, 14, 13, 12 → ? → 7, 6, 5, 4

27 3, 6, 9, 12 → ? → 1, 2, 3, 4

28 4, 6, 8, 10 → ? → 2, 3, 4, 5

29 8, 6, 4, 2 → ? → 11, 9, 7, 5

30 3, 2, 1, 0 → ? → 11, 10, 9, 8

34/ SIMPLE EQUATIONS

If $7 \times \square = 28$, then this is a type of **equation** and $\square$ is being used to show an unknown number.

This equation is only **true** if 4 is written in the box because $7 \times \boxed{4} = 28$.

EXAMPLE

▶ $\square + 8 = 13$

The box needs 5 in it.

$\boxed{5} + 8 = 13$

Exercise 34A

1 $\square - 3 = 2$

2 $\square + 1 = 3$

3 $2 \times \square = 10$

4 $2 + \square = 5$

5 $\square \div 3 = 2$

6 $\square \times 3 = 21$

7 $\square + 7 = 11$

8 $5 \times \square = 30$

9 $35 \div \square = 7$

10 $10 \times \square = 30$

11 $\square \times 4 = 12$

12 $\square - 5 = 5$

13 $24 \div \square = 4$

14 $\square + 2 = 6$

15 $\square \div 3 = 5$

16 $\square \times 2 = 10$

17 $5 - \square = 1$

18 $2 + \square = 6$

19 $\square \div 4 = 2$

20 $\square - 1 = 6$

21 $3 + \square = 8$

22 $\square \times 2 = 12$

23 $7 + \square = 9$

24 $18 \div \square = 6$

25 $\square - 2 = 3$

26 $\square \times 7 = 28$

27 $11 + \square = 19$

28 $16 \div \square = 2$

29 $\square - 6 = 3$

30 $\square \times 10 = 100$

Exercise 34B

1 $9 - \square = 2$	**2** $36 \div \square = 9$	**3** $\square \div 7 = 56$	**4** $\square - 15 = 4$
5 $3 + \square = 15$	**6** $2 \times \square = 14$	**7** $\square + 21 = 33$	**8** $30 \div \square = 5$
9 $19 + \square = 23$	**10** $\square \div 6 = 8$	**11** $\square \times 8 = 32$	**12** $16 - \square = 5$
13 $5 + \square = 12$	**14** $\square \div 4 = 6$	**15** $\square \times 2 = 9$	**16** $\square + 9 = 18$
17 $12 - \square = 2$	**18** $7 + \square = 15$	**19** $\square \div 5 = 8$	**20** $\square \times 7 = 35$
21 $24 - \square = 6$	**22** $4 \times \square = 32$	**23** $\square \div 6 = 7$	**24** $\square + 8 = 13$
25 $12 - \square = 3$	**26** $6 \times \square = 30$	**27** $\square - 4 = 7$	**28** $\square + 9 = 13$
29 $45 \div \square = 9$	**30** $2 \times \square = 7$		

35/ EQUATIONS AND FORMULAE IN WORDS

The area of a rectangle can be found by multiplying the width by the height.

EXAMPLE

▶ What is the area of a rectangle that has a width of 5 cm and a height of 4 cm?

Area = 5 × 4 = 20

The area is 20 cm² (cm² means square centimetres).

EXAMPLE

▶ I think of a number and divide by 3. The answer is 6. What is the number?

18 ÷ 3 = 6

The number is 18.

Exercise 35A

1 I think of a number and add 3. The result is 18. What was the number?

2 A triangle has three equal angles. The total of the angles in a triangle is 180°. What is the size of each angle?

3 I think of a number and multiply it by four. This gives twenty. What was the number?

4 Michelle cuts 18 cm from a length of wood. If this leaves her with 32 cm, how long was the piece of wood?

5 Speed is found by dividing the distance travelled by the time taken. If the speed of a car is 35 m.p.h. over a distance of 140 miles, how long did the journey take?

6 The cost of hiring a mixer is £7 plus a charge for each day it is hired. If the total cost for a day is £15, what is the charge per day?

7 I think of a number and then take away six. If the answer is two, what is the number?

8 The perimeter of a square is found by multiplying the length of a side by four. If the perimeter of a square is 36 cm, what is the length of a side?

9 The temperature has fallen by 6°C and is now 8°C. What was the starting temperature?

10 A quarter of a number is five. What is the number?

11 Sabrina is twice as old as Nigel. If Sabrina is twelve, how old is Nigel?

12 I think of a number and multiply it by 3. This gives 15. What is the number?

13 Mike has used 125 minutes of his tape. He has 55 minutes left. How many minutes does the tape last?

14 I think of a number and add 7. The result is 13. What was the number?

15 The area of a rectangle is found by multiplying the width by the height. If the area is 32 cm^2 and the height is 4 cm, what is the width?

16 I think of a number and add five. The result is twelve. What was the number?

17 Half of an angle is 75°. What is the angle?

18 Gemma is half the age of Mike. If Gemma is eight years old, how old is Mike?

19 I think of a number and double it. This gives 24. What is the number?

20 Jack cuts 25 cm from a length of wood. If this leaves him with 35 cm, how long was the piece of wood?

Exercise 35B

1 A quarter of a number is three. What is the number?

2 The sum of the angles in a triangle is 180°. Two of the angles are of equal size and the other angle is 70°. What is the size of each of the equal angles?

3 A number is doubled and then 3 is added. This gives 13. What is the number?

4 In one year from now Tim will be six and Keith will be twice as old. How old is Keith now?

5 I think of a number and then take away two. If the answer is eight, what is the number?

6 Terry and Pauline share £10 so that Terry has £2 more than Pauline. How much does Pauline receive?

7 I think of a number, double it and add 5 to get 21. What is the number?

8 I think of a number and add 1 to it. I then multiply the total by 2 to give 24. What is the number?

9 Jenny reads some pages of her book. She reads the same number of pages on the second day. On the third day she reads ten pages to bring the total for the three days to 56 pages. How many pages did she read on the first day?

10 The area of a triangle is found by multiplying the base by the height and then dividing by two. If the area is 12 cm^2. and the base is 6 cm, what is the height?

11 A number is multiplied by five to give 35. What is the number?

12 Beckie notes the time that she takes on her homework one weekend. She takes one hour on one subject and then spends half an hour on each of her other subjects. If the total time taken is $2\frac{1}{2}$ hours, how many subjects did she do?

13 Large cans are placed in a wooden box which has a weight of 1 kg. The cans weigh 2 kg each. If the total weight of the box and cans is 17 kg, how many cans are there?

14 I think of a number and subtract 3 before dividing by 2 to get 4. What is the number?

15 Stephen uses 5 spoons of sugar plus 2 spoons for each person. He uses a total of 17 spoons of sugar. How many people were there?

16 I think of a number and add 3. The result is 18. What was the number?

17 In two years time Mark will be five and Matthew will be twice as old. How old is Matthew now?

18 Mr Hull loses three of his chickens. He sells half of those remaining. If he now has five chickens, how many did he have originally?

19 I double a number and add 5. This gives 13. What was the number?

20 The cost of hiring a drill is £3 plus £2 per day. For how many days does Mr Brown hire a drill if the cost is £9?

36/ NAMING POINTS ON GRAPHS

When naming the **coordinates** of a point on a graph, the rule is:

   go ALONG then UP

or

   x coordinate then y coordinate

EXAMPLE

▶ State the coordinates of the points W, X, Y and Z in the diagram.

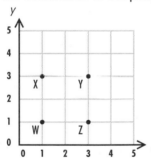

W = (1, 1)   X = (1, 3)

Y = (3, 3)   Z = (3, 1)

Exercise 36A

State the coordinates of each point.

1
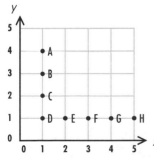

2
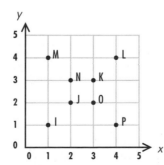

3
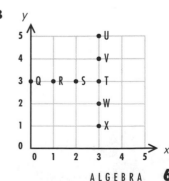

4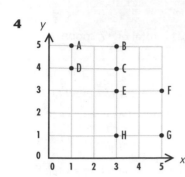

5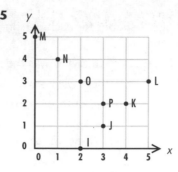

6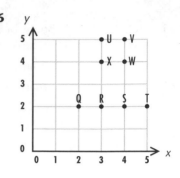

Exercise 36B

State the coordinates of each point.

1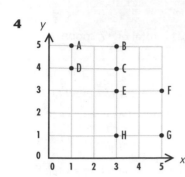

2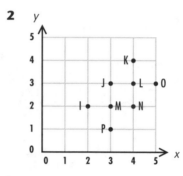

3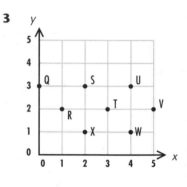

4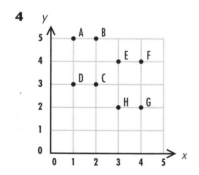

5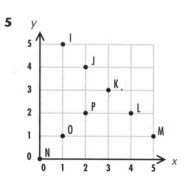

6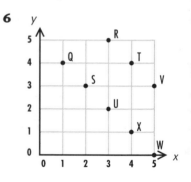

37/ PLOTTING POINTS ON GRAPHS

You will need to draw a 5 × 5 grid, like the one in the diagram, for each of the questions in these exercises.

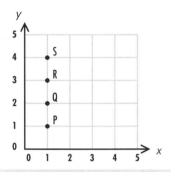

EXAMPLE

▶ Plot and label these points:

P = (1, 1)

Q = (1 ,2)

R = (1, 3)

S = (1, 4)

Exercise 37A

Draw a 5 × 5 grid for each question. Plot and label the points given.

1 A = (1, 1), B = (2, 2), C = (3, 3) and D = (4, 4)
2 E = (4, 4), F = (4, 3), G = (4, 2) and H = (4, 1)
3 I = (0, 2), J = (1, 2), K = (2, 2) and L = (3, 2)
4 M = (1, 5), N = (2, 4), O = (3, 3) and P = (4, 2)
5 Q = (3, 4), R = (3, 3), S = (3, 2) and T = (3, 1)
6 U = (2, 0), V = (3, 1), W = (4, 2) and X = (5, 3)
7 A = (5, 2), B = (2, 2), Y = (2, 3) and Z = (5, 3)
8 C = (0, 3), D = (3, 3), E = (3, 1) and F = (0, 1)
9 G = (0, 5), H = (0, 3), I = (5, 5) and J = (5, 3)
10 K = (1, 1), L = (1, 0), M = (4, 1) and N = (4, 0)

Exercise 37B

Draw a 5 × 5 grid for each question. Plot and label the points given.

1 P = (0, 4), Q = (1, 3), R = (2, 2) and S = (3, 1)
2 T = (0, 4), U = (1, 4), V = (2, 4) and W = (3, 4)
3 X = (1, 0), Y = (2, 0), Z = (3, 0) and A = (4, 0)
4 B = (2, 2), C = (3, 3), D = (4, 4) and E = (5, 5)
5 F = (3, 5), G = (3, 4), H = (3, 3) and I = (3, 2)
6 J = (0, 4), K = (0, 3), L = (0, 2) and M = (0, 1)
7 N = (1, 4), O = (1, 2), P = (5, 2) and Q = (5, 4)
8 R = (1, 1), S = (1, 4), T = (2, 4) and U = (2, 1)
9 W = (0, 3),V = (0, 4), X = (5, 4) and Y = (5, 3)
10 A = (1, 3), B = (2, 2), C = (3, 1) and D = (4, 0)

Exercise 37C

Draw a 5 × 5 grid for each question. Plot the points and join them together as instructed to draw shapes.

1 Join (1, 0) to (1,1) to (1, 2) to (1, 3) to (1, 4).
Join (1, 4) to (2, 4) to (3, 4).
Join (1, 2) to (2, 2) to (3, 2).

2 Join (2, 4) to (3, 4) to (4, 4).
Join (3, 4) to (3, 3) to (3, 2) to (3, 1).

3 Join (2, 5) to (2, 4) to (2, 3) to (2, 2) to (2, 1).
Join (5, 5) to (5, 4) to (5, 3) to (5, 2) to (5, 1).
Join (2, 3) to (3, 3) to (4, 3) to (5, 3).

4 Join (1, 4) to (2, 3) to (3, 2) to (4, 1).
Join (1, 1) to (1, 2) to (1, 3) to (1, 4).
Join (4, 4) to (4, 3) to (4, 2) to (4, 1).

5 Join (0, 3) to (1, 3) to (2, 3) to (3, 3) to (4, 3).
Join (3, 4) to (4, 3).
Join (3, 2) to (4, 3).

6 Join (2, 4) to (3, 4) to (4, 4) to (5, 4)
Join (1, 2) to (1$\frac{1}{2}$, 3) to (2, 4).
Join (4, 2) to (4$\frac{1}{2}$, 3) to (5, 4).
Join (1, 2) to (2, 2) to (3, 2) to (4, 2).

7 Join (1, 4) to (1, 3) to (1, 2) to (1, 1).
Join (1, 1) to (2, 1$\frac{1}{2}$) to (3, 2).
Join (1, 4) to (2, 3$\frac{1}{2}$) to (3, 3).
Join (3, 3) to (3, 2).

8 Join (0, 0) to (1, 2) to (2, 4).
Join (4, 0) to (3, 2) to (2, 4).
Join (1, 2) to (2, 2) to (3, 2).

Exercise 37D

Draw a 5 × 5 grid for each question. Plot the points and join them together as instructed to draw shapes.

1 Join (1, 4) to (1, 3) to (1, 2) to (1, 1).
Join (1, 1) to (2, 1) to (3, 1).

2 Join (1, 1) to (2, 2) to (3, 3) to (4, 4).
Join (1, 4) to (2, 3) to (3, 2) to (4, 1).

3 Join (2, 5) to (3, 5) to (4, 5).
Join (2, 5) to (2, 4) to (2, 3).
Join (2, 3) to (3, 3) to (4, 3).
Join (4, 3) to (4, 2) to (4, 1).
Join (2, 1) to (3, 1) to (4, 1).

4 Join (2, 5) to (3, 5) to (4, 5).
Join (2, 2) to (2, 1).
Join (3, 5) to (3, 4) to (3, 3) to (3, 2) to (3, 1).
Join (2, 1) to (3, 1).

5 Join (1, 4) to (1, 3) to (1, 2) to (1, 1).
Join (3, 5) to (3, 4) to (3, 3) to (3, 2).
Join (1, 1) to (2, 1$\frac{1}{2}$) to (3, 2).
Join (1, 4) to (2, 4$\frac{1}{2}$) to (3, 5).

6 Join (2, 5) to (2, 4) to (2, 3) to (2, 2) to (2, 1).
Join (2, 3) to (3, 2) to (4, 1).
Join (2, 3) to (3, 4) to (4, 5).

7 Join (0, 2) to (1, 2) to (2, 2) to (3, 2).
Join (3, 2) to (4, 3) to (5, 4).
Join (3, 2) to (4, 1) to (5, 0).

8 Join (1, 5) to (2, 5) to (3, 5).
Join (1, 1) to (2, 1) to (3, 1).
Join (1, 3) to (2, 3) to (3, 3).
Join (1, 1) to (1, 2) to (1, 3).
Join (3, 3) to (3, 4) to (3, 5).

38/ ROMAN NUMERALS

Here are some of the important conversions:

I	1	X	10	C	100
II	2	XX	20	D	500
III	3	XXX	30	M	1000
IV	4	XL	40		
V	5	L	50		
VI	6	LX	60		
VII	7	LXX	70		
VIII	8	LXXX	80		
IX	9	XC	90		

EXAMPLE

▶ Convert 1649 to Roman numerals.

1000	=	M
600	=	DC
40	=	XL
9	=	IX
1649	=	MDCXLIX

EXAMPLE

▶ Convert MCMXCV to normal numerals.

M	=	1000
CM	=	900
XC	=	90
V	=	5
MCMXCV	=	1995

Exercise 38A

Convert to Roman numerals.

1. 16 XVI
2. 23 XXXIII
3. 45 XLV
4. 34 XXXIV
5. 28 XXVIII
6. 75 LXXV
7. 69 LXIX
8. 150 CL
9. 200 CC
10. 405 CCCCVR
11. 370 CCCLXX
12. 610 DCX
13. 700 DCC
14. 850 DCCCL
15. 824 DCCCXXIV
16. 248 CCXLVIII
17. 674 DCCIV
18. 1066 MLXVI
19. 1812 MDCCCXII
20. 1975 MDCCCCLXXV

Exercise 38B

Convert to Roman numerals.

1. 25 XXV
2. 17 XVII
3. 19 XIV
4. 33 XXXXIII
5. 46 XLVI
6. 39 XXXIX
7. 27 XXVII
8. 92 XCII
9. 112 CXII
10. 300 CCC
11. 271 CCLXXI
12. 155 CLV
13. 750 DCCL
14. 553 DLIII
15. 390 CCCXC
16. 149 CLXLX
17. 299 CCXCIX
18. 1089 MLXXXIX
19. 1815 MDCCCXV
20. 1990 MDCCCCXC

Exercise 38C

Convert to normal numerals.

1 XII 12 **2** VIII 8 **3** XVII 17 **4** XLI 41 **5** LI 51

6 XXX 30 **7** XXIX 29 **8** LXXI 6671 **9** XV 15 **10** XXVI 26

11 CCCXX 320 **12** DX 510 **13** XXVIII 28 **14** XXXV 35 **15** LX 60

16 DCCC 800 **17** XLVIII 188 48 **18** MM 2000 **19** MCMLXXXI 1900 1000 900 80 **20** CMXXV 925

Exercise 38D

Convert to normal numerals.

1 IV 4 **2** XI **3** XXI **4** XIV **5** VII

6 XXV **7** IX **8** XLIII **9** XIX **10** LXXXIV

11 LXIII **12** CCXXX **13** CXL **14** CXXX **15** DLV

16 DCC **17** CDXXV **18** CM **19** MD **20** MCMXC 1990

REVISION

Exercise C

1 State the next two terms in each number pattern.
   (a) 1, 3, 5, 7, 9, 11
   (b) 8, 11, 14, 17, 20, 23
   (c) 25, 21, 17, 13, 9, 5
   (d) 7, 12, 17, 22, 27, 32

2 State the *output* for each of the given inputs:
   (a) in → ×2 → +3 → out (i) 5 (ii) 7 (iii) 9 (iv) 23
       (i) 1 (ii) 2 (iii) 3 (iv) 10
   (b) in → ×3 → −1 → out (i) 2 (ii) 5 (iii) 11 (iv) 29
       (i) 1 (ii) 2 (iii) 4 (iv) 10

3 State the function (?) required to give the outputs from the inputs.
   (a) 9, 8, 7, 6 → ? → 5, 4, 3, 2 −4
   (b) 2, 4, 6, 8 → ? → 3, 5, 7, 9 +1
   (c) 1, 3, 5, 7 → ? → 2, 6, 10, 14 ×2
   (d) 3, 2, 1, 0 → ? → 7, 5, 3, 1

4 Find the value for ☐ in each of the following:
   (a) ☐ − 2 = 3 5 (b) ☐ + 3 = 12 9
   (c) 2 × ☐ = 12 6 (d) ☐ ÷ 3 = 4 12

5 State the coordinates of the points plotted.

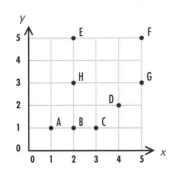

6 Draw a 5 × 5 grid for each question (as shown in question 5). Plot and label the points:
   (a) A = (1, 1), B = (2, 2), C = (3, 3) and D = (4, 4)
   (b) E = (2, 4), F = (3, 4), G = (4, 4) and H = (5, 4)
   (c) I = (1, 1), J = (1, 2), K = (1, 3) and L = (1, 4)
   (d) M = (1, 1), N = (2, 4), P = (3, 3) and Q = (4, 2)

7 Convert the following to Roman numerals:
   DXCVIII
   (a) 36 XXXVI (b) 55 LV   (c) 219 CCXIX (d) 598 DXC   (e) 1745

8 Convert these Roman numerals to normal numerals:
   (a) XXI 21   (b) XV 25 15 (c) XCV 95   (d) CCCXXXIII   (e) MCMXXVIII

Exercise CC

1 Tom finds a series of numbers: 7, 10, 13, 16, 19. If 7 is the first term and 10 is the second term, state the 6th, 7th, 9th and 11th terms.

2 The 7th term of a series is 21, the 6th term is 19 and the 5th term is 17. State the first two terms of the series.

3 (a) A function machine doubles the input and adds five. State the output for each of the following inputs: 3, 5, 7 and 10.
   (b) Another function machine adds five and then doubles. What outputs does it give for the same inputs. Does it give the same outputs as the first function machine?

4 A function machine adds three and then multiplies by four. State the output for an input of 4. What would be the input to get an output of 40?

5 I think of a number and double it. I then subtract a certain amount.
   (a) If I think of 5 as my number, the answer that I get is 7. What is the amount that I subtract?
   (b) What number do I start with if my answer is 21?

6 Joe cuts 25 cm from a length of wood. If this leaves him with 47 cm, how long was the piece of wood?

7 Two bags of nuts and four packets of crisp weigh 200 grams. The crisps weigh 25 grams each. What is the weight of each packet of nuts?

8 Some medicine must be taken at the rate of two tablets three times a day for the first day. After that the dose is reduced to one tablet three times a day.
(a) Nick takes the tablets for six days. How many tablets does he take in total?
(b) Sanjay takes a total of 30 tablets. For how many days did Sanjay take the tablets?

9 State the coordinates of the points plotted.

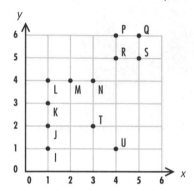

10 Plot the points on a 6 × 6 grid and join them together to draw a shape.
(a) Join (1, 5) to (2, 4) to (3, 3).
   Join (3, 0) to (3, 1) to (3, 2) to (3, 3).
   Join (5, 5) to (4, 4) to (3, 3).
(b) Join (2, 5) to (3, 5) to (4, 5) to (5, 5).
   Join (2, 2) to (3, 2) to (4, 2) to (5, 2).
   Join (5, 5) to (5, 4) to (5, 3) to (5, 2).
   Join (2, 5) to (2, 4) to (2, 3) to (2, 2).
   Join (3, 3) to (4, 3) to (4, 4) to (3, 4).

11 Zoe reads the date on a memorial stone. The year is given as MCMXVIII. What year is this?

12 A building is completed in 1994. This year is to be written on a metal plate in Roman numerals. How should this be written?

Shape, space and measures

39/ DIFFERENT SHAPES

In this diagram, shape b is the odd one out because it has four sides. All the other shapes have three sides.

These shapes can be sorted in various ways:

3 straight sides	4 straight sides	No curved edges	Includes a right angle
b, c	a, d	a, b, d, g	b, c, g

Exercise 39A

For each question write down
(a) which shape is the odd one out,
(b) why the odd one out is different from all the other shapes.

1

2

3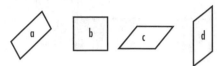

4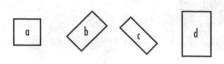

5

6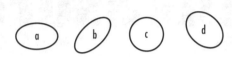

7

8

Exercise 39B

For each question write down
(a) which shape is the odd one out,
(b) why the odd one out is different from all the other shapes.

1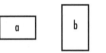

2

3

4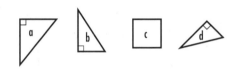

5

6

7

8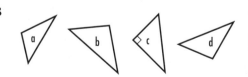

Exercise 39C

Copy and complete the table. Write the letter of each shape in any suitable column.

Includes a right angle	3 sides	4 sides	Some curved sides

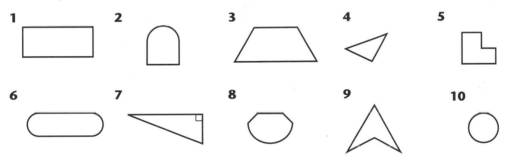

1 **2** **3** **4** **5**

6 **7** **8** **9** **10**

Exercise 39D

Copy and complete the table in Exercise 39C. Write the letter of each shape in any suitable column.

1 **2** **3** **4** **5**

6 **7** **8** **9** **10**

Exercise 39E

Copy and complete the table. Write the letter of each solid in any suitable column.

Some straight edges	Some curved edges	Includes a right angle

1 **2** **3** **4** **5**

6 **7** **8** **9** **10**

Exercise 39F

Copy and complete the table in Exercise 39E. Write the letter of each shape in any suitable column.

1

2

3

4

5

6

7

8

9

10

40/ MEASURING LENGTHS

The line below has been measured using millimetres and centimetres.

Length = 37 mm = 3.7 cm

The line below has first been measured in centimetres *and* millimetres; this measurement can then be expressed as a length in centimetres alone.

Length = 8 cm 2 mm = 8.2 cm

Exercise 40A

Measure each of the following lines.

1 ————————

2 ——————————

3 ————

4 ——

5 ——————————

6 ——

7 —

8 ——————————

9 ——————————

10 ——————————————

11 ————————

12 ——————

13 ————

14 ——————————————

15 ——————

16 ——————————

17 ————————————————

18 ————————————————

19 ——————————————

20 ——————————————

Exercise 40B ───────────────────────────────────

Measure each of the following lines.

1 ────────────────   2 ─────   3 ──

4 ──────   5 ─────────   6 ──

7 ────────────   8 ────────   9 ───────────────

10 ─────────────────   11 ─────   12 ──────────

13 ─────────────────────   14 ────   15 ──────────────────

16 ───────────────   17 ──────────────────────

18 ──────────────────

19 ────────────────────

20 ────────────────

41/ DRAWING LINES

EXAMPLE

▶ Draw lines of lengths (a) 2.6 cm (b) 43 mm (c) 5.2 cm.

(a) ──────────

(b) ───────────────

(c) ────────────────

Exercise 41A ───────────────────────────────────

Draw a line for each of these lengths.

1	5.7 cm	**2**	1.4 cm	**3**	9.1 cm	**4**	16 mm	**5**	6.3 cm
6	41 mm	**7**	2.5 cm	**8**	53 mm	**9**	5.1 cm	**10**	9.7 cm
11	3.2 cm	**12**	38 mm	**13**	8.5 cm	**14**	43 mm	**15**	2.9 cm
16	60 mm	**17**	7.3 cm	**18**	8.3 cm	**19**	17 mm	**20**	4.9 cm
21	11.4 cm	**22**	15.6 cm	**23**	117 mm	**24**	12.1 cm	**25**	212 mm
26	14.2 cm	**27**	199 mm	**28**	16.8 cm	**29**	17.4 cm	**30**	154 mm

Draw a line for each of these lengths.

1	3.1 cm	**2**	1.0 cm	**3**	26 mm	**4**	6.5 cm	**5**	75 mm
6	1.8 cm	**7**	7.4 cm	**8**	52 mm	**9**	2.2 cm	**10**	9.0 cm
11	42 mm	**12**	6.8 cm	**13**	3.6 cm	**14**	28 mm	**15**	6.4 cm
16	3.4 cm	**17**	84 mm	**18**	5.8 cm	**19**	4.6 cm	**20**	79 mm
21	128 mm	**22**	145 mm	**23**	13.5 cm	**24**	18.1 cm	**25**	17.9 cm
26	18.3 cm	**27**	16.7 cm	**28**	173 mm	**29**	206 mm	**30**	11.5 cm

42/ ACCURATE DRAWINGS

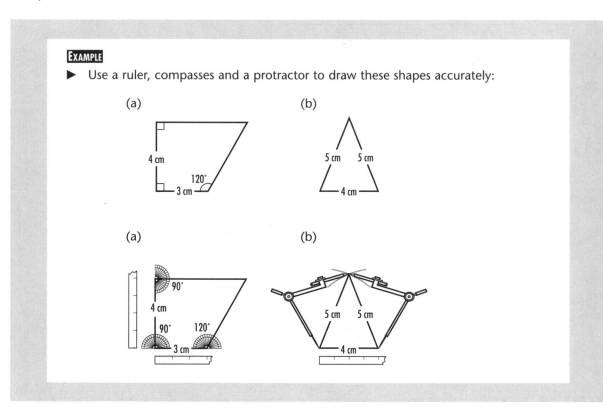

EXAMPLE

▶ Use a ruler, compasses and a protractor to draw these shapes accurately:

Draw these shapes accurately using a ruler, protractor and, if necessary, compasses.

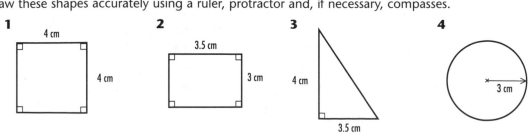

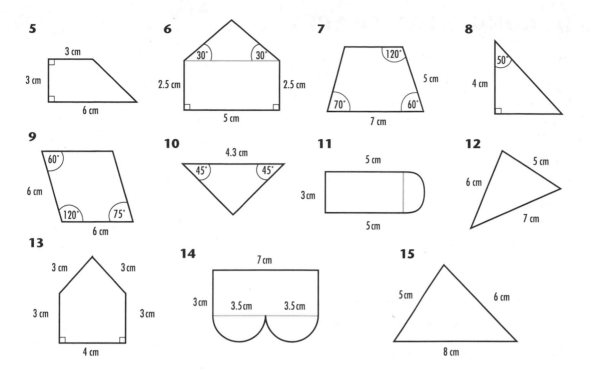

Exercise 42B

Draw these shapes accurately using a ruler, protractor and, if necessary, compasses.

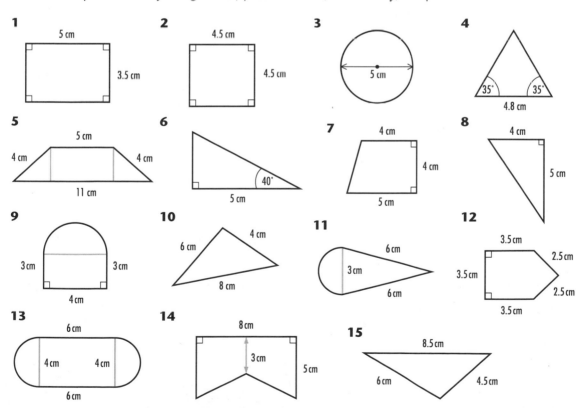

43/ CONGRUENT SHAPES

Two shapes are **congruent** if they are identical.

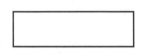

These two shapes are congruent.
The shapes are in different positions but are still identical and so are congruent.

One rectangle is slighter larger than the other.
They are *not* congruent.

Exercise 43A

Write down whether each pair of shapes is congruent, or not congruent.

1

2

3

4

In each question write down the letters of the two shapes which are congruent.

5

6

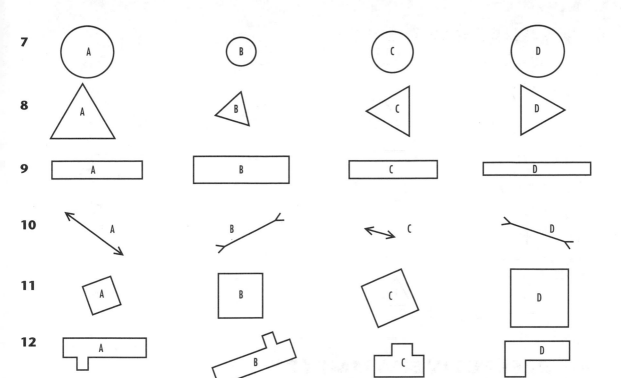

7 A   B   C   D

8 A   B   C   D

9 A   B   C   D

10 A   B   C   D

11 A   B   C   D

12 A   B   C   D

Exercise 43B

Write down whether each pair of shapes is congruent, or not congruent.

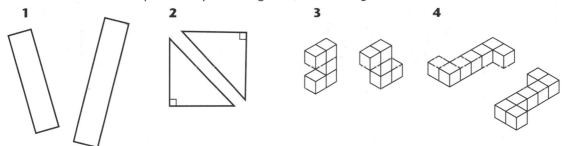

1   2   3   4

In each question write down the letters of the two shapes which are congruent.

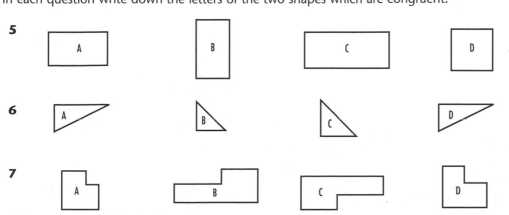

5 A   B   C   D

6 A   B   C   D

7 A   B   C   D

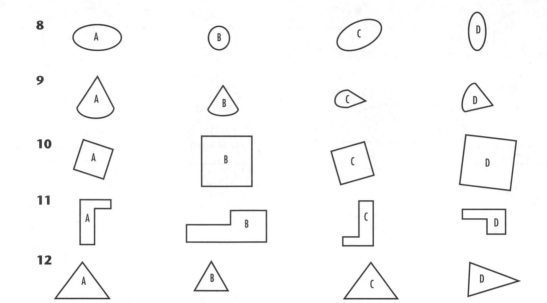

8 A B C D

9 A B C D

10 A B C D

11 A B C D

12 A B C D

44/ **REFLECTIVE SYMMETRY**

This shape has **reflective symmetry**. The left-hand side is a reflection of the right-hand side.

← mirror line or line of symmetry

This shape does *not* have reflective symmetry.

Exercise 44A

Does each shape have reflective symmetry? Answer YES or NO for each shape.

1   **2**   **3**   **4**   **5**

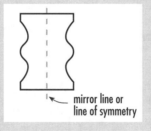

6   **7**   **8**   **9**   **10**

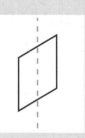

Exercise 44B

Does each shape have reflective symmetry? Answer YES or NO for each shape.

1   **2**   **3**   **4** 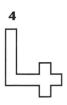   **5**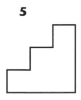

6   **7**   **8** 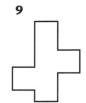   **9** 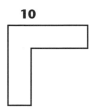   **10**

Exercise 44C

For each question copy the shape and (a) draw in all possible lines of symmetry, (b) write down the number of possible lines of symmetry.

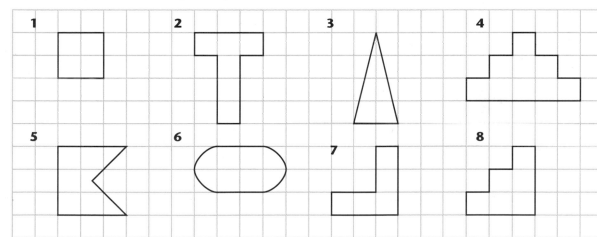

9   **10**   **11** 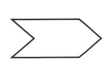   **12**

13   **14**   **15**

Exercise 44D

For each question copy the shape and (a) draw in all possible lines of symmetry, (b) write down the number of possible lines of symmetry.

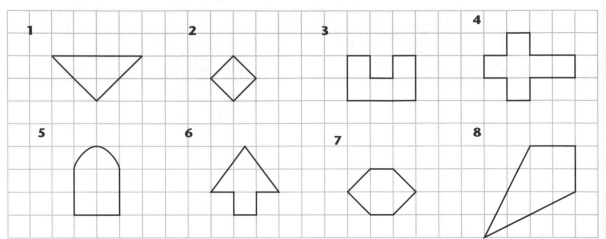

1 **2** **3** **4**

5 **6**  **7** **8**

9 **10** **11** **12**

13 **14** **15**

45/ **REFLECTION**

EXAMPLE

▶ Copy and complete each diagram by drawing the reflection in the mirror line.

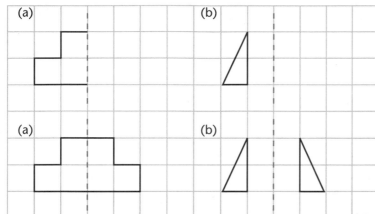

Exercise 45A

Copy and complete each diagram by drawing the reflection in the mirror line(s).

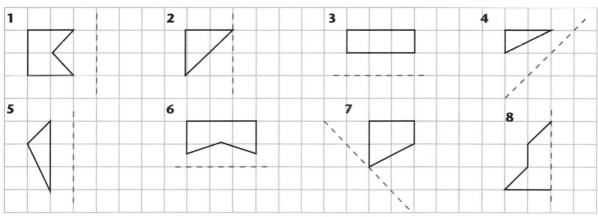

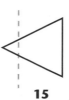

Exercise 45B

Copy and complete each diagram by drawing the reflection in the mirror line(s).

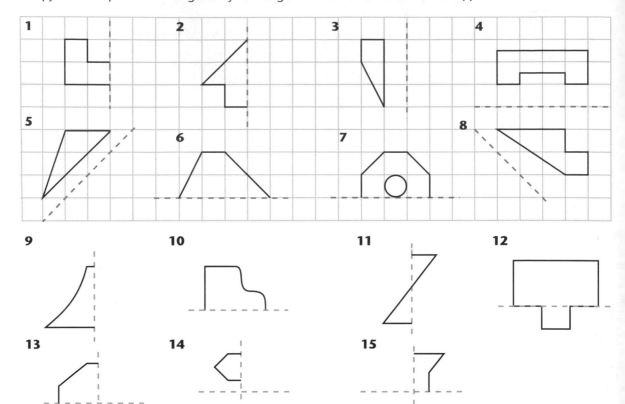

46/ ROTATIONAL SYMMETRY

The number of times a shape fits on top of itself as it turns through one revolution about a point (the centre of rotation) is called the **order** of rotation.

A shape has **rotational symmetry** if its order of rotation is greater than 1. Shape (c) does *not* have rotational symmetry.

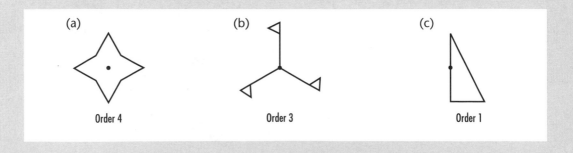

Exercise 46A

(a) Write down the question numbers of the diagrams which do *not* have rotational symmetry about the point shown.

(b) For those diagrams with rotational symmetry write down the order.

1

2

3

4

5

6

7

8

9
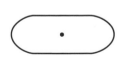

10

11

12

Exercise 46B

(a) Write down the question numbers of the diagrams which do *not* have rotational symmetry about the point shown.

(b) For those diagrams with rotational symmetry write down the order.

1

2

3

4

5

6

7

8

9

10

11

12

REVISION

Exercise D

1 Copy and complete the table.
   Write the letter of each shape in any suitable column of the table (there could be more than one).

Includes a right angle	Some curved edges	Some straight edges

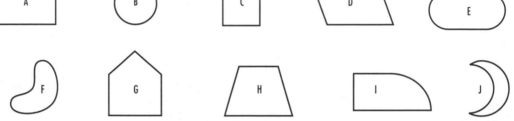

2 Measure each of the following lines. Give your answers in centimetres.

(a) ————————————————   (b) ————————————————

(c) ————   (d) ——————————   (e) ————————————————

(f) ——————————————   (g) ————————   (h) ————————————————————

(i) ————————————————   (j) ——————————

3 Draw lines for each of these lengths:

(a) 3.2 cm   (b) 4.6 cm   (c) 65 mm   (d) 2.7 cm   (e) 53 mm
(f) 7.3 cm   (g) 38 mm   (h) 5.9 cm   (i) 6.8 cm   (j) 4.7 cm

4 Draw these shapes using a ruler, protractor and compasses as necessary.

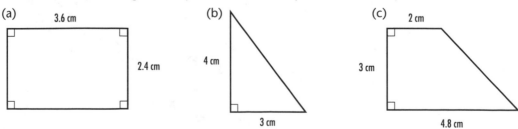

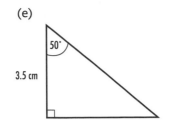

(d)

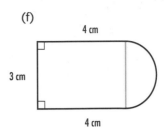

(e)

(f)

5 In each group of shapes identify the two which are congruent.

(a)

 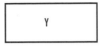 

W   X   Y   Z

(b)

W   X   Y   Z

(c)

W   X   Y   Z

(d)

W   X   Y   Z

6 In each case copy the diagram and (i) draw in all the possible lines of symmetry, (ii) write down the number of possible lines of symmetry.

(a)   (b)   (c)   (d)   (e)

  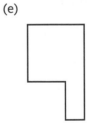

7 Copy and complete each diagram by drawing the reflection in the mirror line(s).

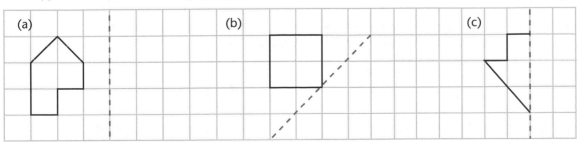

(a)   (b)   (c)

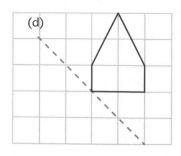
(d)

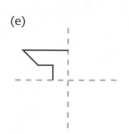
(e)

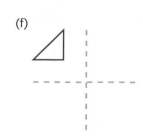
(f)

8   For each diagram write down the order of rotational symmetry about the point shown.

(a)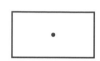

(b)

(c)

(d)

(e)

(f)

(g)

(h)

47/ UNITS

These are some of the units of measure in common use.

Length
Metric: millimetres (mm), centimetres (cm), metres (m), kilometres (km)
Imperial: inches (in), feet (ft), yards (yd), miles (m)

Capacity
Metric: millilitres (ml), centilitres (cl), litres (*l*)
Imperial: pints (pt), gallons (gal), fluid ounces (fl. oz)

Weight
Metric: milligrams (mg), grams (g), kilograms (kg), tonnes (t)
Imperial: ounces (oz), pounds (lb), stones (st), tons (t)

Exercise 47A

Write down the common units you would use to make the measurements listed below.
In each case give both (a) the metric and (b) the Imperial unit.

1   The thickness of your exercise book

2   The weight of a cup of tea

3   The distance from London to Paris

4   The height of a door

5   The length of a car

6   The amount of water in a kitchen sink

7   The weight of a bag of cement

8   The width of the blackboard

9	The capacity of a drinking mug	**10**	The weight of a £1 coin
11	The length of an ant	**12**	The length of your arm
13	The capacity of a milk pan	**14**	Your own weight
15	The weight of an elephant	**16**	The height of Mount Everest
17	The width of a pencil	**18**	The weight of a human hair
19	The capacity of a kettle	**20**	The amount of fluid in a tablespoon

Exercise 47B

Write down the common units you would use to make the measurements listed below.
In each case give both (a) the metric and (b) the Imperial unit.

1	The distance across a town	**2**	An amount of medicine
3	The weight of a brick	**4**	The length of a finger nail
5	The amount of water in a garden pond	**6**	The weight of a pencil
7	The length of a pencil	**8**	The weight of a indoor plant
9	The capacity of a bath	**10**	Your height
11	The height of a house	**12**	The distance from school to home
13	The capacity of a tea cup	**14**	The weight of a car
15	The length of your textbook	**16**	The length of a swimming pool
17	The weight of a drop of ink	**18**	The capacity of a washing-up bowl
19	The weight of a box of corn flakes	**20**	The distance from Land's End to John o' Groats

48/ ESTIMATION

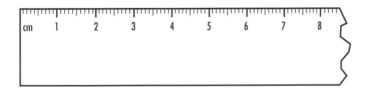

Exercise 48A

Using the ruler above as a guide, estimate in centimetres:

1	The length of your textbook	**2**	The length of your pen
3	The width of your table	**4**	The height of the door
5	The height of the window	**6**	Your hand span

Estimate the following:

7	The distance from your elbow to your fingertips	**8**	The length of a double-decker bus
9	The width of your shoes	**10**	The width of a football pitch
11	The distance across a bicycle wheel	**12**	The capacity of a milk pan
13	The weight of this textbook	**14**	The capacity of a hot-water bottle
15	The capacity of an egg cup	**16**	The weight of a packet of corn flakes

17 The capacity of a can of fizzy drink   **18** The weight of a pint of milk

19 The weight of four bath towels   **20** The capacity of a drinking mug

Exercise 48B

Using the ruler above as a guide, estimate in centimetres:

1 The width of your textbook   **2** The height of your table

3 The length of your table   **4** Your height

5 The height of the top of the board   **6** The length of your index finger

Estimate the following:

7 The width of your thumb   **8** The height of a double-decker bus

9 The length of your shoes   **10** The width of a swimming pool

11 The height of a tennis net   **12** The capacity of a bath

13 The weight of a tin of beans   **14** The capacity of a milk bottle

15 The capacity of a washing-up bowl   **16** The weight of a pint of water

17 The weight of an iron   **18** The capacity of a tea cup

19 The weight of ten exercise books   **20** The weight of a kettle

49/ SCALES AND DIALS

Scales and dials are used to take measurements. Some can be read exactly, whilst others may require some estimation.

EXAMPLE

▶ Write down the measurement shown on each of these scales.

(a)   (b)

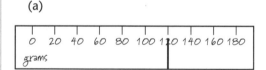 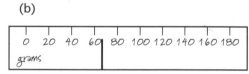

(a) The pointer is exactly on 120 g.
(b) The pointer is between 60 g and 80 g. An estimate could be 66 g.

Exercise 49A

Write down the measurement shown on each of these scales.

1   **2**

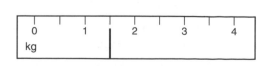

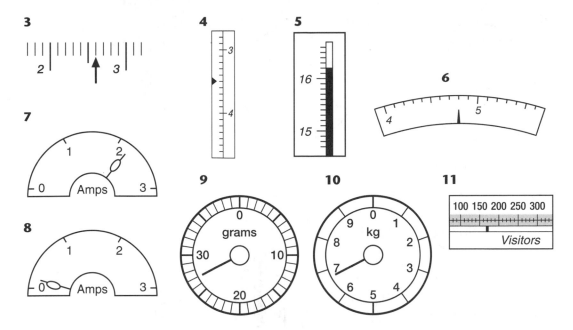

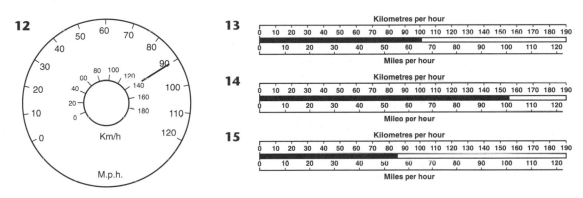

Give the speed in (a) kilometres per hour (b) miles per hour.

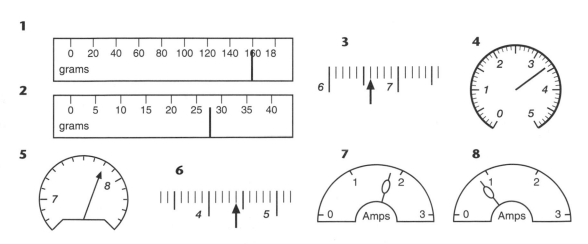

Exercise 49B

Write down the measurement shown on each of these scales.

9

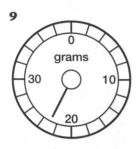

10

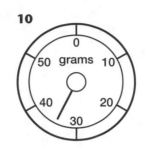

11

Give the temperature in (a) °C (b) °F.

12

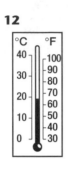

13

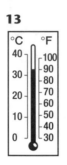

14

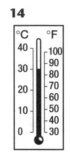

15

50/ **TIME**

This time is written as 6.45 in figures, or
'a quarter to seven' in words.

Exercise 50A

Write these times (a) in figures (b) in words.

1

2

3

4

5

6

7

8

9

10

Exercise 50B

Write these times (a) in figures (b) in words.

1   **2**   **3**   **4**   **5**

6   **7**   **8**   **9**   **10**

On the 24-hour clock:
a time before noon, such as 8.30 a.m., is written as 0830 hours;
a time after noon, such as 9.45 p.m., is written as 2145 hours.

Exercise 50C

Change these 12-hour clock times to 24-hour clock times.

1 9 a.m.	**2** 10.30 a.m.	**3** 11.15 a.m.	**4** 3.40 p.m.
5 6.20 p.m.	**6** 8.10 a.m.	**7** 12.40 p.m.	**8** 8.45 p.m.
9 5.25 p.m.	**10** 3.15 p.m.	**11** 2.30 p.m.	**12** 7.25 a.m.
13 11.30 a.m.	**14** 11.55 a.m.	**15** 9.15 p.m.	

Change these 24-hour clock times to 12-hour clock times.

16 1255 hours	**17** 1110 hours	**18** 0810 hours	**19** 0025 hours
20 0740 hours	**21** 2335 hours	**22** 1415 hours	**23** 1035 hours
24 0855 hours	**25** 0920 hours	**26** 2225 hours	**27** 2055 hours
28 1816 hours	**29** 1725 hours	**30** 1320 hours	

Exercise 50D

Change these 12-hour clock times to 24-hour clock times.

1 9.50 a.m.	**2** 10.15 a.m.	**3** 12.15 p.m.	**4** 2.25 p.m.
5 10.10 p.m.	**6** 7.20 a.m.	**7** 9.35 a.m.	**8** 1.15 p.m.
9 8.30 a.m.	**10** 11.25 p.m.	**11** 2.50 p.m.	**12** 12.50 p.m.
13 1.50 a.m.	**14** 0020 a.m.	**15** 12.20 p.m.	

Change these 24-hour clock times to 12-hour clock times.

16	0255 hours	**17**	1210 hours	**18**	0010 hours	**19**	1430 hours
20	2350 hours	**21**	0054 hours	**22**	0730 hours	**23**	0330 hours
24	1310 hours	**25**	0820 hours	**26**	1345 hours	**27**	0342 hours
28	2214 hours	**29**	0917 hours	**30**	1327 hours		

Exercise 50E

Give the time in either 12- or 24-hour time as indicated in the question.

1   5 hours before 0230 hours

2 $4\frac{1}{2}$ hours before 3.30 p.m.

3 $3\frac{1}{4}$ hours before 1430 hours

4 $1\frac{1}{2}$ hours before 10.35 p.m.

5 $3\frac{3}{4}$ hours after 2.40 a.m.

6 $5\frac{1}{2}$ hours after 1130 hours

7 $2\frac{1}{4}$ hours before 0515 hours

8   16 hours before 2.00 a.m.

9   1 h 20 min after 2.15 p.m.

10   3 h 40 min before 1450 hours

11   2 h 10 min before 2205 hours

12   4 h 25 min after 5.45 a.m.

Work out how long it is between these times.

13   8.50 a.m. to 10.15 a.m.

14   0830 to 0920

15   1345 to 0115

16   12.15 a.m. to 2.35 p.m.

17   0917 to 1427

18   1.30 p.m. to 4.45 p.m.

19   0342 to 2314

20   1422 to 1615

21   1505 to 1942

22   0135 to 2305

23   2.45 p.m. to 6.10 p.m.

24   1.34 p.m. to 10.30 p.m.

25   3.50 a.m. to 8.10 a.m.

Exercise 50F

Give the time in either 12- or 24-hour time as indicated in the question.

1   3 hours before 7.15 a.m.

2 $2\frac{1}{2}$ hours before 0355 hours

3 $4\frac{1}{4}$ hours after 2.20 p.m.

4 $5\frac{1}{2}$ hours after 0715 hours

5   7 hours before 1340 hours

6   12 hours after 0740 hours

7 $6\frac{1}{2}$ hours before 1820 hours

8 $5\frac{3}{4}$ hours before 1.15 p.m.

9   4 hours after 2.55 p.m.

10 $2\frac{1}{4}$ hours before 2020 hours

11 $3\frac{1}{2}$ hours after 0125 hours

12 $4\frac{1}{4}$ hours after 11.35 a.m.

Work out how long it is between these times.

13   0915 to 1325

14   8.50 a.m. to 11.05 a.m.

15   0840 to 1235

16   3.35 p.m. to 8.15 p.m.

17   1035 to 1720

18   2105 to 2350

19 1.15 p.m. to 7.21 p.m.

20 10.30 a.m. to 1.40 p.m.

21 1455 to 2015

22 0615 to 2235

23 9.25 a.m. to 6.40 p.m.

24 10.30 a.m. to 3.40 p.m.

25 1150 to 1555

51/ AREA AND PERIMETER

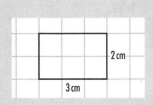 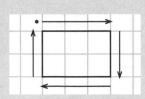

The **perimeter** of any shape is the distance all the way around the outside.

Perimeter = 3 + 2 + 3 + 2

           = 10 cm

The **area** of any shape is a measure of the surface contained within the shape.

Area = 6 cm^2

The perimeter is a length, and is measured in mm, cm, m, km etc.

The area is a measure of surface, and is measured in mm^2, cm^2, m^2, km^2 etc.

Exercise 51A

Find (a) the perimeter (b) the area of each shape.

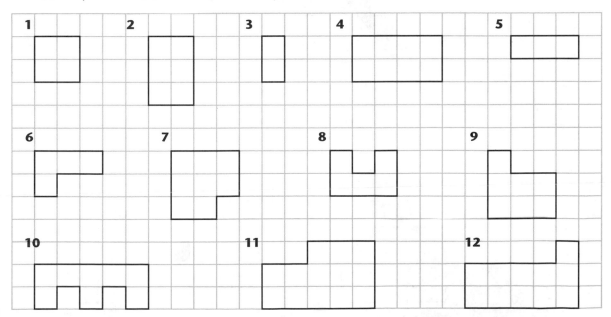

Draw these diagrams on a squared grid to help you find (a) the perimeter (b) the area of each shape.

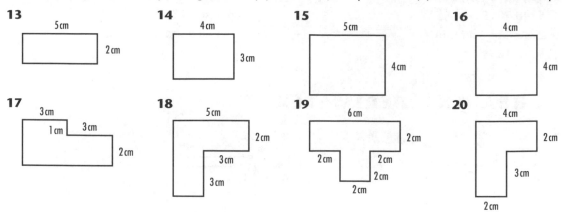

13
5 cm
2 cm

14
4 cm
3 cm

15
5 cm
4 cm

16
4 cm
4 cm

17
3 cm
1 cm   3 cm
2 cm

18
5 cm
2 cm
3 cm
3 cm

19
6 cm
2 cm
2 cm   2 cm
2 cm
2 cm

20
4 cm
2 cm
3 cm
2 cm

Exercise 51B

Find (a) the perimeter (b) the area of each shape.

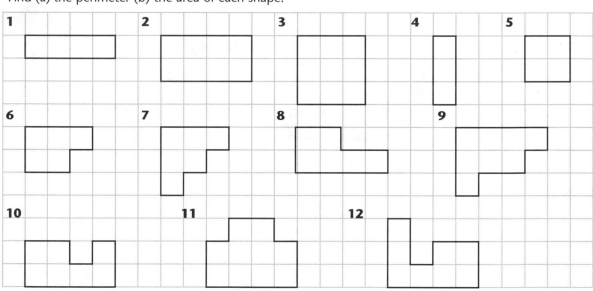

1   **2**   **3**   **4**   **5**

6   **7**   **8**   **9**

10   **11**   **12**

Draw these diagrams on a squared grid to help you find (a) the perimeter (b) the area of each shape.

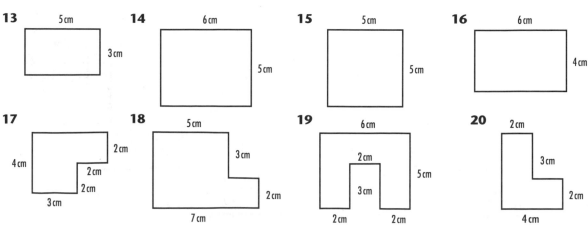

13
5 cm
3 cm

14
6 cm
5 cm

15
5 cm
5 cm

16
6 cm
4 cm

17
4 cm
2 cm
2 cm
2 cm
3 cm

18
5 cm
3 cm
2 cm
7 cm

19
6 cm
2 cm
5 cm
3 cm
2 cm   2 cm

20
2 cm
3 cm
2 cm
4 cm

52/ VOLUME

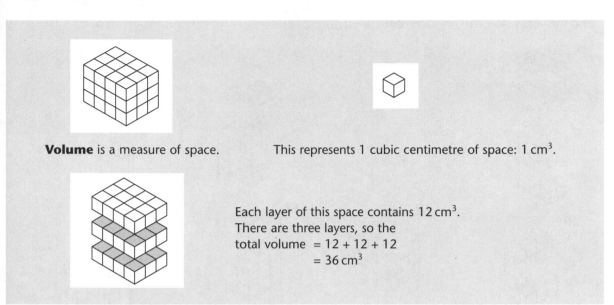

Volume is a measure of space.

This represents 1 cubic centimetre of space: 1 cm³.

Each layer of this space contains 12 cm³.
There are three layers, so the
total volume = 12 + 12 + 12
            = 36 cm³

Exercise 52A

Find the volume, in cm³, of each of these solids.

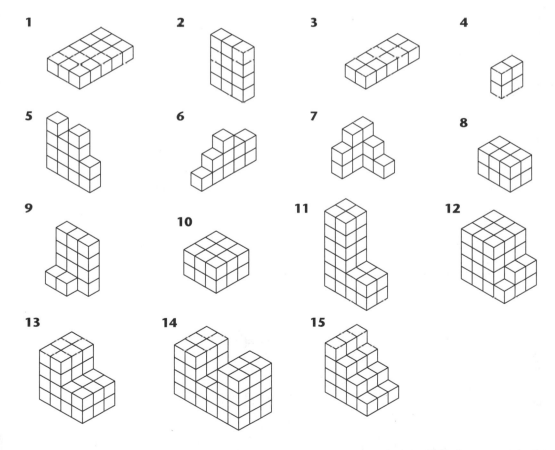

1 **2** **3** **4**

5 **6** **7** **8**

9 **10** **11** **12**

13 **14** **15**

Exercise 52B

Find the volume, in cm³, of each of these solids.

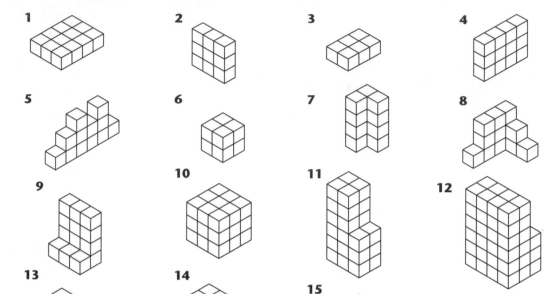

REVISION

Exercise E

1 Write down the common metric units you would use to make the measurements described below.

(a) The weight of a cat

(b) The capacity of a tea cup

(c) The height of a child

(d) The length of a garden path

(e) The width of your pencil

(f) The weight of a car

(g) The capacity of a hot-water bottle

(h) The weight of a pencil

2 Write down the measurement shown on each of these scales.

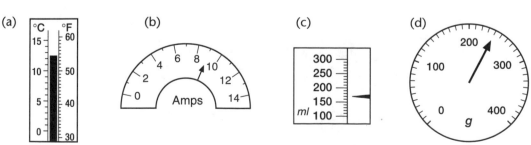

(e) 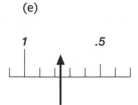 (f) 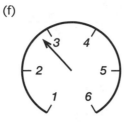 (g)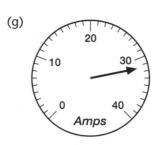

3 Write down these times (i) in figures (ii) in words.

(a)   (b)   (c)   (d)   (e)

4 Change these 12-hour clock times to 24-hour clock times.

(a) 7.40 a.m.　　　(b) 5.30 p.m.　　　(c) 4.25 a.m.　　　(d) 8.55 p.m.　　　(e) 11.05 p.m.

5 Change these 24-hour clock times to 12-hour clock times.

(a) 0140 hours　　　(b) 1330 hours　　　(c) 1010 hours　　　(d) 2205 hours　　　(e) 1515 hours

6 Work out how long it is between these times.

(a) 1345 and 1550　　　(b) 7.30 a.m. and 11.50 a.m.　　　(c) 0720 and 1640

(d) 1055 and 1420　　　(e) 6.36 a.m. and 4.15 p.m.

7 Find (i) the perimeter (ii) the area of each shape.

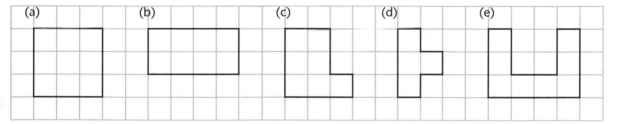

8 Find the volume of these solids.

 = 1 cm³

(a) 　(b) 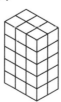　(c) 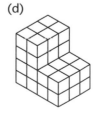　(d) 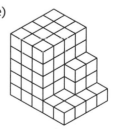　(e)

Exercise EE ————————————————————————————————

1   This is a bus timetable.

BOLTON, Bus Station	0620	0650	0715		1615	1700	1730
Farnworth, King Street Bus Station	0635	0705	0733	AND	1633	1718	1748
Walkden, Stocks Hotel	0641	0711	0740	EVERY	1640	1725	1755
Swinton, Civic Centre	0650	0720	0750	30	1650	1735	1805
Irlams o'th' Height	0657	0727	0757	MINUTES	1657	1742	
Pendleton Precinct	0705	0735	0805	UNTIL	1705	1750	
MANCHESTER, Arndale bus Station	0720	0750	0820		1720	1805	

(a) How many buses leave Bolton between 0715 and 1615 (excluding 0715 and 1615)?

(b) How long does it take the 0620 Bolton bus to get to Pendleton Precinct?

(c) How long does it take the 1725 Walkden bus to get to Manchester Arndale?

(d) Penny lives in Farnworth. What is the time of the latest bus she can catch to arrive in Pendleton by 0915?

(e) Which bus arrives in Walkden just before 5.30 p.m.?

2   This floor is being fitted with black and white carpet tiles, each 1 cm square.

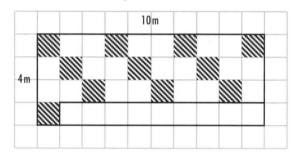

(a) How many more tiles are needed on the bottom row?

(b) What is the area of the floor?

(c) Once complete, how many white tiles will there be?

(d) How many black tiles will there be?

(e) What is the perimeter of the floor?

3   This is a plan of a hotel room.

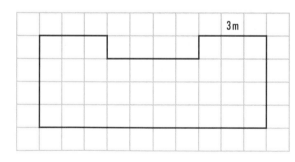

(a) What is the area of the floor?

(b) What is the perimeter of the room?

(c) Skirting board costs £3.50 per metre. How much will it cost to put new skirting board around the edge of the room?

Handling data

53/ USING TABLES

Exercise 53A

Write down the cost of the following holidays.

1. Seven nights self catering from 5 July
2. Seven nights self catering from 11 May
3. Fourteen nights half board from 12 September
4. Seven nights half board from 5 July
5. Fourteen nights self catering from 21 June
6. Fourteen nights half board from 15 June
7. Seven nights half board from 13 August
8. Fourteen nights self catering from 28 July

NORIDA BEACH
– Self catering/Half board

Prices are in £s per
full fare paying passenger

Departures on or between	Self catering		Half board	
	7 nights	14 nights	7 nights	14 nights
1 MAY – 10 MAY	229	239	299	419
11 MAY – 18 MAY	239	259	319	429
19 MAY – 23 MAY	249	319	329	469
24 MAY – 30 MAY	329	329	409	489
31 MAY – 7 JUNE	279	319	369	499
8 JUNE – 20 JUNE	289	339	379	509
21 JUNE – 4 JULY	299	359	389	549
5 JULY – 14 JULY	309	379	429	589
15 JULY – 20 JULY	329	399	439	609
21 JULY – 7 AUG	349	429	459	639
8 AUG – 20 AUG	319	399	429	609
21 AUG – 30 AUG	319	389	429	599
31 AUG – 11 SEPT	309	369	419	579
12 SEPT – 18 SEPT	299	349	409	529
19 SEPT – 25 SEPT	279	309	369	469
26 SEPT – 5 OCT	259	299	339	449
6 OCT – 11 OCT	249	289	329	439
12 OCT – 31 OCT	259	259	359	439

89F 735 ASE Lachs, 75T £11995	91H 325 SE 4dr Granite 35T ... £15995
93L 530 Auto Touring Avus 7T. £30995	93L 320 Coupe, Sterling 8T £20495
88F 535 SE, Black, 60T £10995	93L 320 Auto 4dr, Brilliant, 9T . £19495
93K 530 V8 Diamond, 19T .. £25995	93K 320 Lagoon 4dr 17T £17495
94L 525 SE Fjord, 7T £23995	92K 320 4dr SE Lagoon 24T ... £17495
93L 525 ASE, Orient, 13T £23995	91J 320 4dr SE Sterling 35T ... £15495
92K 525 X Tour SE Lazer 23T . £23995	91H 320 4dr Alpine 11T £14995
92J 525 ASE, Brilliant 41T £17795	92K 318iS Granite 26T £16995
91J 525 Sport, Diamond, 54T . £16995	92J 318i 4dr, Diamond 30T £13995
90H 525 SE, Sterling, 43T £14995	91J 318i 4dr Calypso 28T £13495
94L 520 SE Fjord 8T £20995	91J 318i 4dr Auto Calypso 28T £14495
92K 520 SE Calypso 8T £17995	93L 316i 4dr Calypso 7T £15395
93K 518 SE Sterling 23T £15995	92K 316i 4dr Sterling 11T £14295
92K 518 SE Alpine 20T £14995	91J 316i 4dr Mauritius 38T £12495
93K 325 Coupe Diamond 16T . £22995	91J 316i 4dr Brilliant 27T £12295
92K 325 Auto Coupe 24T £23495	89F 320 Cony Alpine 36T £11995
91J 325 4dr SE Lagoon 40T ... £16995	94L 316i Auto Touring Lux 9T . £11295
91J 325 SE 4dr Alpine 30T £17995	90H 316i Touring Brill 27T £11295

Find the cost of the following cars.

9. 92K 518 SE Alpine 20T
10. 91J 316i 4dr Brilliant 27T
11. 93K 320 Lagoon 4dr 17T
12. 88F 535 SE, black, 60T
13. A 1992 car under £14000
14. The oldest car listed in the table
15. The most expensive car
16. A 'Diamond' car which was registered in 1991

Item no.	Cat. no.	Description	Cutting width	Motor power	Safety lock-off switch	Auto stop	Cable length (m)	No. of cutting heights	Metal/ plastic blades	Grass collection	Stripes lawn	Cutting method	OUR PRICE
1	730/1544	Flymo Chevron RE300	12 inch	900 Watt	●	●	15	5	Metal	●	●	Rotary	£99.50
2	730/1702	Flymo VenturerTurbo 350	14 inch	1400 Watt	●	●	20	7	Metal	●	●	Rotary	£149.50
3	730/1427	Flymo Minimo E25	10 inch	750 Watt	●		16	3	Plastic			Hover	£49.50
4	730/1458	Flymo E30	12 inch	900 Watt	●		15	3	Metal			Hover	£69.50
5	730/1489	Flymo Sprintmaster XE250	10 inch	900 Watt	●	●	15	4	Metal	●		Hover	£99.50
6	730/1506	Flymo Sprintmaster XE3000	12 inch	1150 Watt	●	●	15	4	Metal	●		Hover	£119.50
7	730/1317	Flymo Hovervac HV3000	12 inch	1200 Watt	●	●	15	4	Metal	●		Hover	£129.50
8	730/1678	Flymo Hovervac Turbo Compact 350	14 inch	1300 Watt	●	●	20	4	Metal	●		Hover	£139.50
9	730/1513	Flymo Hovervac HV4000	16 inch	1500 Watt	●	●	20	4	Metal	●		Hover	£149.50
10	730/1582	Flymo Lawnchief RL400	16 inch	3.5hp Petrol			N/A	6	Metal	●		Rotary	£199.50

Write down the catalogue numbers of the following lawnmowers.

17 A lawnmower which is under £50

18 A lawnmower which costs more than £150

19 A hover mower with a 16-inch cutting width

20 A 900-watt mower with an auto stop and a 10-inch cutting width

21 A lawnmower with plastic blades

22 A mower with 15 m of cable and a 10-inch cutting width

23 A 900-watt mower with an auto stop and a 12-inch cutting width

24 A mower with 20 m of cable, a 14-inch cutting width, and which stripes the lawn

25 A 900-watt mower without an auto stop

Exercise 53B

Write down the cost of the following holidays.

1 Fourteen nights bed and breakfast from 19 May

2 Fourteen nights self catering from 19 September

3 Seven nights bed and breakfast from 8 June

4 Fourteen nights bed and breakfast from 15 July

5 Seven nights self catering from 15 August

6 Seven nights self catering from 15 June

7 Fourteen nights bed and breakfast from 4 September

8 Seven nights bed and breakfast from 15 August

MARIETTA – Self catering/Bed & breakfast

Prices are in £s per full fare paying passenger

Departures on or between	Self catering		Bed & breakfast	
	7 nights	14 nights	7 nights	14 nights
1 MAY – 10 MAY	199	259	199	259
11 MAY – 18 MAY	219	269	219	269
19 MAY – 23 MAY	249	339	249	339
24 MAY – 30 MAY	309	359	309	359
31 MAY – 7 JUNE	269	329	269	329
8 JUNE – 20 JUNE	319	369	319	369
21 JUNE – 4 JULY	309	379	309	379
5 JULY – 14 JULY	319	409	319	409
15 JULY – 20 JULY	339	429	339	429
21 JULY – 7 AUG	349	459	349	459
8 AUG – 20 AUG	339	449	339	449
21 AUG – 30 AUG	329	429	329	429
31 AUG – 11 SEPT	309	389	309	389
12 SEPT – 18 SEPT	299	369	299	369
19 SEPT – 25 SEPT	289	339	289	339
26 SEPT – 5 OCT	259	279	259	279
6 OCT – 11 OCT	229	249	229	249
12 OCT – 31 OCT	249	249	249	249

Number of monthly repayments	12				36				60			
EXAMPLES OF LOAN AMOUNTS	Monthly Repayments		Total Repayable		Monthly Repayments		Total Repayable		Monthly Repayments		Total Repayable	
	PPI	−PPI	PPI	−PPI	PPI	−PPI	PPI	−PPI	PPI	−PPI	PPI	−PPI
£10000	957.12	905.83	11485.44	10869.96	383.87	350.28	13819.32	12610.08	275.78	239.17	16546.80	14350.20
£7500	717.85	679.38	8614.20	8152.56	287.91	262.71	10364.76	9457.56	206.83	179.38	12409.80	10762.80
£5000	478.57	452.92	5742.84	5435.04	191.94	175.14	6909.84	6305.04	137.88	119.58	8272.80	7174.80
£3000	287.14	271.75	3445.68	3261.00	115.16	105.08	4145.76	3782.88	82.73	71.75	4963.80	4305.00
£2000	191.99	181.67	2303.88	2180.04	77.38	70.56	2785.68	2540.16	55.82	48.33	3349.20	2899.80
£1000	95.99	90.83	1151.88	1089.96	38.69	35.28	1392.84	1270.08	27.91	24.17	1674.60	1450.20
£500	48.00	45.42	576.00	545.04	19.35	17.64	696.60	635.04	13.95	12.08	837.00	724.80

Repayments for a loan *can* include PPI (Personal Payment Insurance) or *not* include PPI. Find the following.

9 The total repayments with PPI on a £5000 loan over 36 months

10 The total repayments without PPI on a £1000 loan over 12 months

11 The monthly repayments with PPI on a £500 loan over 60 months

12 The total repayments with PPI on a £3000 loan over 12 months

13 The monthly repayments without PPI on a £10000 loan over 60 months

14 The monthly repayments with PPI on a £500 loan over 36 months

15 The total repayments without PPI on a £2000 loan over 12 months

16 The monthly repayments without PPI on a £7500 loan over 36 months

Description	No. of digits	Total no. of functions	Scientific functions	Programmable steps	Formula entry	Wallet/case	No. of data memories	Physical constants	Complex numbers	Fraction facility	Direct algebraic logic	Statistical functions	Number bases	Parenthesis (levels)	Logic operations	Root solver	"GCSE" suitable	"A" Level suitable	Linear regression	Hyperbolic	Power	OUR PRICE
CASIO FX82LB	8 + 2	135	116			Hard case	1	2		●		●		18			●			●	Batt	£6.75
TEXAS TI-30X	10 + 2	84	75			Hard case	3			●	AOS	●		15			●			●	Batt	£7.50
SHARP EL531GH	10 + 2	152	145		●	Case	1		●	●	●	●		15			●			●	Batt	£7.75
TEXAS TI-36X	10 + 2	164	158			Hard case	3	8		●	AOS	●	●	15	●		●	●	●	●	Solar	£10.99
CASIO FX95	10 + 2	140	118			Hard case	1	2		●		●		18			●			●	Batt	£10.75
SHARP EL520G	10 + 2	176	153		●	Hard case	1		●	●	●	●	●	15			●	●		●	Batt/Solar	£12.75
CASIO FX115D	10 + 2	236	181			Soft case	7	2	●	●		●	●	18		●	●	●	●	●	Batt/Solar	£14.75
CASIO FX570D	10 + 2	268	213			Wallet	7	32	●	●		●	●	18	●		●	●	●	●	Batt	£14.75
SHARP EL556G	10 + 2	276	259		●	Case	7	32	●	●		●	●	15			●	●	●	●	Batt	£16.75
CASIO FX992V	12 + 2	350	295			Wallet	7	128	●	●		●	●	18	●		●	●	●	●	Batt/Solar	£17.75
TEXAS TI-67	10	210	176	1536	●	Hard case	1536	10	●	●	EOS			16	●	●	●	●	●	●	Batt	£17.75
CASIO FX6300G	11	324	217	400		Hard case	26-78	2	●	●		●	●	10	●		●	●	●	●	Batt	£32.50
TEXAS TI-81	16 + 8	300	151	2400	●	Hard case	4632			●	EOS			16			●	●	●	●	Batt	£49.50
SHARP EL9300	16×8	437	161	20K		Case	32K		●	●	●	●	●	15	●		●	●	●	●	Batt	£59.00
CASIO FX7700G	16×8	386	206	4164		Hard case	26-548	2	●	●		●	●	26	●		●	●	●	●	Batt	£67.50
TEXAS TI-82	16×8	550	190	28200	●	Hard case	32K			●	EOS		MEM		●	●	●	●	●	●	Batt	£74.50
TEXAS TI-85	21×8	1500	1200	28600	●	Hard case	32K	15	●	●	EOS		●	MEM	●	●		●	●	●	Batt	£89.00

Write down the cost of the calculator with the following features.

17 A calculator in a wallet

18 A calculator with formula entry under £10

19 A solar-powered calculator in a soft case

20 A calculator which is not suitable for GCSE

21 A calculator with complex numbers and a root solver, but under £50

22 A solar-powered calculator with formula entry

23 A calculator with 18 parenthesis levels but no number bases

24 A calculator with logic operations and complex numbers, but no formula entry

25 A calculator with no fraction facility

Exercise 54A

LEIGH, Bus Station	0825	0925	1025		1825	1925	2025	2125	2225
Astley, Straits	0837	0937	1037	AND	1837	1937	2037	2137	2237
Boothstown, Simpson Road	0843	0943	1043	EVERY	1843	1943	2043	2143	2243
Worsley, Court House	0848	0948	1048	HOUR	1848	1948	2048	2148	2248
Swinton, Partington Lane	0854	0954	1054	UNTIL	1854	1954	2054	2154	2254
Pendleton, Church	0902	1002	1102		1902	2002	2102	2202	2302
MANCHESTER, Arndale Bus Station	0914	1014	1114		1914	2014	2114	2214	2314

1 At what time does the 1037 bus from Astley arrive in Pendleton?

2 At what time does the 2043 bus from Boothstown arrive in Manchester?

3 At what time does the 2225 bus from Leigh arrive in Swinton?

4 How long does it take the 0848 bus from Worsley to travel to Pendleton?

5 How long does it take the 1825 bus from Leigh to travel to Manchester?

6 How long does it take the 2237 bus from Astley to travel to Swinton?

7 Tracey needs to catch a bus from Worsley to Manchester to arrive no later than 2200. At what time is the latest bus she can catch?

8 William catches the 1337 bus from Astley. At what time does it arrive in Manchester?

9 Barbara lives in Boothstown and wants to travel to Pendleton to arrive by 12 noon. At what time is the latest bus she can catch?

10 Ali needs to be in Swinton by 10.45 a.m. At what time is the latest bus he could catch from Astley?

Mondays to Fridays	🍴 ✕	🍴 ✕	🍴 PS A	🍴 PS A	🍴 PS A	🍴 ✕	🍴 ✕	🍴	🍴 ✕	🍴 ✕
Manchester Piccadilly	0520	0600	0645	0710	0730	0830	0833	0930	1030	1033
Stockport	0528	0608	0654	0718	0738	0842	0842	0938	1038	1042
Wilmslow	0536	—	—	0727	—	—	0850	—	1046	1050
Crewe	0557	—	—	—	—	—	0925	—	—	1125
Macclesfield	—	0622	0706	—	0752	0852	—	0952	—	1039g
Stoke-on-Trent	—	0642	0727	—	0812	0912	—	1012	—	1102g
Rugby	—	0730	—	—	—	—	1023	—	—	1223
Milton Keynes Central	—	0824	—	—	0924	—	1049	—	1221	1247
Watford Junction	—	0856	—	0921s	1013	1045s	1129	1142s	1313	1329
London Euston	0813	0840	0916	0944	1011	1108	1136	1205	1307	1334

11 At what time does the 0600 train from Manchester arrive in London?

12 At what time does the 0838 train from Stockport arrive at Watford?

13 At what time does the 1125 train from Crewe arrive at Milton Keynes?

14 How long does it take the 0608 train from Stockport to travel to Rugby?

15 How long does it take the 0830 train from Manchester to travel to London?

16 How long does it take the 1125 train from Crewe to travel to Milton Keynes?

17 Brian lives in Stockport and needs to get to London by 12 noon. What is the time of the latest train from Stockport that he could catch?

18 Samantha wants to catch the latest train she can from Wilmslow to be in Watford by 11.00 a.m. At what time does the train that she should catch leave Wilmslow?

19 June wants to get to Stoke by 9.00 a.m. What is the time of the latest train from Manchester that she could catch?

20 Sandeep is on the 0930 train from Manchester to London. The train is delayed by 1 h 45 min because of engine failure. At what time will it arrive?

MANCHESTER, Piccadilly		0635	0722	0732	0752	0757	0822	0852		1752	1830	1933	2030	2130	2230	2330
Blackfriars Bridge		0640	0728	0737	0758	0807	0828	0858		1758	1835	1938	2035	2135	2235	2335
Pendleton Precinct	arr.		0738				0808	0838	0908		1808						
Pendleton Precinct	dep.	0648	0740	0745	0810	0810	0840	0910	AND	1810	1843	1946	2043	2143	2243	2343
Hope Church		0653	0747	0750	0817	0815	0847	0917	EVERY	1817	1848	1951	2048	2148	2248	2348
Ellesmere Park		0658	0752	0755	0822	0820	0852	0922	30	1822	1853	1956	2053	2153	2253	2353
Monton		0703	0758	0800	0828	0825	0858	0928	MINS	1828	1858	2001	2058	2158	2258	2358
Peel Green, New Lane		0710	0807	0807	0837	0834	0907	0937	UNTIL	1837	1905	2008	2105	2205	2305	0005
BROOKHOUSE											1908	2011	2108	2208	2308	0008

1 At what time does the 0732 bus from Manchester arrive in Monton?

2 At what time does the 2143 bus from Pendleton arrive in Peel Green?

3 At what time does the 0822 bus from Manchester arrive in Pendleton Precinct?

4 How long does it take the 0745 bus from Pendleton to travel to Peel Green?

5 How long does it take the 2035 bus from Blackfriars Bridge to travel to Brookhouse?

6 How long does it take the 1752 bus from Manchester to travel to Monton?

7 Linda needs to be at Peel Green by 9.00 a.m. and wants to catch the latest bus that she can from Blackfriars Bridge. At what time will she need to catch her bus?

8 Dipak lives in Pendleton and has an appointment in Ellesmere Park at 8.30 p.m. What is the time of the latest bus that he could catch?

9 Amanda is staying near Hope Church, and wants to travel back home to Brookhouse to arrive no later than 11.00 p.m. What is the time of the latest bus she could catch?

10 Bill would like to catch a bus from Manchester Piccadilly which will get him to Peel Green by 1303. At what time will his bus leave Piccadilly?

11 At what time does the 1745 train from Bristol Temple Meads arrive at London Paddington?

12 At what time does the 1827 train from Bath arrive at Reading?

13 At what time does the 1944 train from Weston-super-Mare arrive at Swindon?

Mondays to Fridays	ICS	ICS	ICS	ICS	ICS	ICS	ICS	IH	IH	IH
Weston-super-Mare	—	1613	1655	—	1736	—	1810	—	1944	2041
Bristol Temple Meads	—	1715	1745	—	1815	—	1915	—	2015	2125
Bristol Parkway ‡	1700	—	—	1800	—	1900	—	2000	—	—
Bath Spa	—	1727	1757	—	1827	—	1927	—	2027	2137
Chippenham	—	1738	1808	—	1838	—	1938	—	2038	2148
Swindon	1730	1754	1824	1830	1855	1928	1955	2029	2055	2205
Didcot Parkway	1746	—	1840	—	1912	—	2012	2046	—	2222
Reading →	1804	1823	1856	1903	1930	1958	2031	2105	2126	2241
Slough	1837	1849	1924	1930	1954	2023	2057	2144	2213	2255
London Paddington	1835	1855	1930	1935	2000	2030	2105	2140	2200	2320

14 How long does it take the 1715 train from Bristol Temple Meads to travel to Reading?

15 How long does it take the 1757 train from Bath to travel to Didcot?

16 How long does it take the 1900 train from Bristol Parkway to travel to London Paddington?

17 Paul needs to travel from Bath to London to arrive no later than 2100. What is the time of the latest train that he could catch?

18 Vera lives in Chippenham. She would like to catch a train to arrive in Didcot no later than 1930. What is the time of the latest train she could catch?

19 Sean needs to arrive in Swindon no later than 1900. What is the time of the latest train that he should catch from Bristol Parkway?

20 Mary needs to travel from Bristol Parkway to Didcot making a change of trains at Swindon. She leaves Bristol Parkway at 1800. What is the earliest time she could get to Didcot?

55/ MAKING FREQUENCY TABLES

► Put the data below into a frequency table.

3	4	3	1	2	3
2	4	2	0	4	0
1	3	4	2	2	3
0	1	2	3	4	3
1	3	3	0	4	2

Number	Tally	Frequency
0	IIII	4
1	IIII	4
2	ЖІІ II	7
3	ЖІІ IIII	9
4	ЖІІ I	6
	Total	30

Exercise 55A

In each question draw and complete a frequency table to summarise the data.

1 The number of matches in a box:

42	38	41	39	40	42	38	40	41	41	39	40
39	41	38	40	40	39	40	38	42	41	39	40
40	39	42	41	38	39	40	39	42	38	41	

2 The vowels found in a paragraph of text:

i	a	e	o	o	u	a	o	e	e	i	a
u	e	o	i	e	o	o	u	a	e	e	i
u	a	e	a	u	e	i	a	i	e	o	o
a	i	e	a								

3 Numbers thrown using a dice:

3	1	4	2	5	6	5	5	3	3	5	4
2	2	1	6	3	2	4	6	3	5	1	3
2	5	3	1	4	6	3	4	2	6	1	5

4 The number of brothers or sisters of each pupil in a class:

2	0	4	1	5	3	5	2	2	3	4	0
2	1	3	4	2	1	3	0	5	1	3	0
2	2	3	1	2	4						

5 The registration letters of cars in an executive car-park:

V	W	S	U	R	T	V	S	W	R	V	V
U	U	S	W	V	T	U	V	S	W	R	T
V	S	U	W	W	T	V	U	T	U	S	W
T	V	R	U								

6 The number of breakdowns of each lorry in a haulage company:

2	0	3	1	2	2	3	4	0	4	2	1
1	3	2	4	2	5	0	3	1	2	2	1
1	5	0	2	1	3	3	0	4	1	2	4

7 The number of defects in a batch of components:

5	2	6	7	3	4	7	6	5	4	3	3
4	5	5	5	7	3	4	4	5	6	2	4
5	4	7	6	6	3	5	6				

8 The number of guinea pigs in a litter:

3	1	4	5	5	6	1	5	2	4	6	5
4	2	5	6	1	4	3	3	4	5	3	5
3	4	5	2	3	3	5	1	6	3	4	

9 The number of deliveries made by a van over a number of days:

8	6	6	8	4	9	9	4	9	6	5	7
8	9	7	4	8	9	5	8	6	7	6	6
5	7	7	6	9	7	5	5	7	6	7	7
8	5	6	6	4	6	8	5	6			

10 The ages of the first forty children to leave a school:

15	11	16	12	14	15	14	13	11	14	16	12
15	11	13	14	11	15	12	14	15	13	11	12
12	11	13	16	12	13	16	12	16	13	14	12
15	14	11	12								

Exercise 55B

In each question draw and complete a frequency table to summarise the data.

1 The number of sweets in a packet:

26	23	27	24	25	24	26	24	23	25	25	23
26	27	24	25	25	25	24	26	25	23	25	26
24	24	25	23	26	27						

2 The shoe size worn by each pupil in a class:

6	4	8	3	6	5	7	4	4	6	3	4
5	4	6	5	8	6	6	4	7	5	3	5
4	6	6	5	4	7						

3 The times six pupils, A, B ,C, D, E and F, are late in a month:

B	A	D	B	B	E	C	A	F	D	A	E
B	D	D	D	E	A	B	F	C	F	B	E
D	A	D	B	C	A	F	B	E	D		

4 The goals scored by teams in a football league:

2	0	3	1	4	0	1	1	3	0	2	1
0	2	3	5	0	1	2	4	3	0	0	1
3	2	0	1								

5 The number of eggs laid by hens at a farm:

1	4	2	0	3	3	4	5	1	1	3	2
2	5	1	3	3	2	3	2	2	0	5	4
1	3	3	5	2	1	4	3	1	1	4	3
2	3	4	2								

6 The number of fish caught by a group of fishermen:

5	1	4	2	2	6	3	6	5	4	4	3
5	4	6	3	4	3	3	4	1	5	5	2
6	5	4	5	4	6	3	4	6	5	5	3
4	3	6	2								

7 In a year group there are six forms called A, E, L, P, S and W. The first forty pupils arriving at a school have their form noted:

L	A	P	E	S	L	L	W	E	E	P	S
A	S	S	W	A	P	L	W	S	A	S	L
L	E	P	L	W	L	E	S	W	P	W	E
L	A	L	S								

8 The price (in pence) charged for a protractor at several shops:

10	14	14	9	12	13	10	10	13	11	12	13
13	14	12	12	10	11	14	9	13	11	13	9
11	10	12	9	12	14	14	11	11	13	10	9
11	10	13	12	11							

9 The number of minutes that the local train service is late over a period of time:

3	3	1	2	5	4	4	6	1	2	5	5
1	1	5	6	2	2	1	3	4	1	6	5
2	1	4	3	1	2	2	4	1	4	1	

10 The number of pints of milk left at each of the houses in the road:

2	3	5	6	4	1	3	5	2	2	6	5
6	2	5	3	2	2	1	4	3	1	2	4
4	5	1	2	3	3	4	5	2	2	2	6
3	2	4	1	3	2	5	1	2			

56/ BAR CHARTS

Exercise 56A

1 The bar chart shows the various ways that the pupils in class 9W came to school.

(a) How many came by car?

(b) How many either walked or cycled?

(c) How many pupils are there in class 9W?

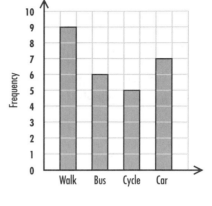

2 The bar chart shows the number of cars parked at a health centre each day at noon.

(a) How many cars were parked during the week?

(b) How many cars were parked on Monday and Tuesday?

(c) On which day was the smallest number of cars parked?

(d) On which day was the largest number of cars parked?

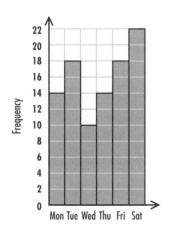

3 The bar chart shows the number of various newspapers delivered one morning.

(a) Which paper was received by the most people?

(b) How many newspapers where delivered?

(c) How many people received the Times or the Telegraph?

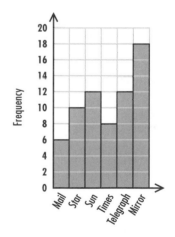

4 The bar chart shows the value of the sales (in £1000s) in a shop over several months.

(a) What was the value of the sales in June?

(b) Which two months had the same sales figure?

(c) Which month had the greatest sales figure?

(d) What is the difference between the greatest and smallest sales figures?

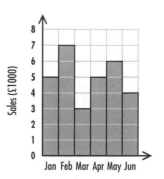

5 The bar chart shows the highest temperature recorded in March in each of various cities.

(a) Which was the warmest town?

(b) Which was the coolest town?

(c) Which two towns share the same maximum temperature?

(d) How much warmer is it in Edinburgh than in Manchester?

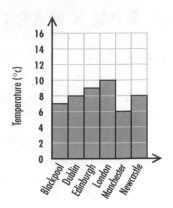

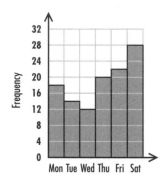

6 The bar chart shows the number of people using a café between 12 noon and 1 p.m. in a week.

(a) On which day was the café busiest?

(b) How many people used the café on (i) Monday (ii) Wednesday (iii) Sunday?

(c) On which day was the café used the least?

7 The bar chart shows the shoe sizes worn by pupils at a school.

(a) How many pupils wear size 5 shoes?

(b) How many pupils wear shoes of size 7 or 8?

(c) How many pupils wear shoes of size 5 or smaller?

(d) How many pupils are there altogether?

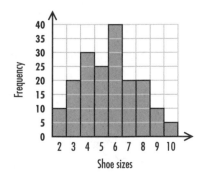

8 The bar chart shows the number of questions attempted by seven pupils in an afternoon.

(a) Who attempted the most questions?

(b) Who attempted the smallest number of questions?

(c) Which two pupils attempted the same number of questions?

(d) How many questions were attempted by Brian?

(e) How many questions were attempted by Ali?

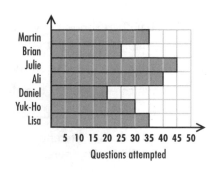

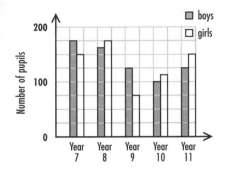

9 The bar chart shows the number of pupils in each of five year groups.

(a) In which year groups are there more boys than girls?

(b) How many pupils are there altogether in (i) Year 7 (ii) Year 10?

(c) Which year group has the fewest pupils?

(d) Which year group has the smallest number of boys?

10 The bar chart shows the sales of a company in England and Wales over a four-month period.

(a) In which month were the maximum sales in England?

(b) In which month were the minimum sales in Wales?

(c) What was the total value of the sales in February, in £1000s?

(d) In which months were the sales in Wales the same?

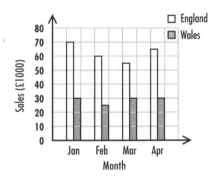

Exercise 56B

1 The bar chart shows the number of pupils present in the class on each day in a week.

(a) On which day were the most pupils present?

(b) How many pupils were present on (i) Tuesday (ii) Friday?

(c) On which two days did the same number of pupils attend?

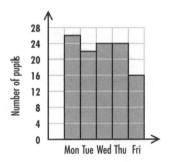

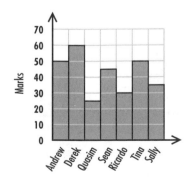

2 The bar chart shows the marks which have been gained in a test by seven pupils.

(a) Who has gained the most marks?

(b) Which two pupils have achieved the same mark?

(c) Which pupils have achieved fewer marks than Sally?

(d) How many marks have been gained by (i) Tina (ii) Sean?

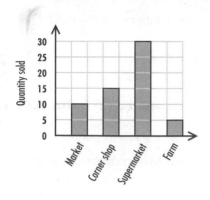

3 The bar chart shows the various places where people buy their fresh vegetables.

(a) How many people buy from the corner shop?

(b) Which is the most popular place for buying vegetables?

(c) How many people buy from the farm?

(d) What is the total number of people who were questioned in the survey?

4 The bar chart shows the amounts collected for charity by six form groups.

(a) Which group collected the smallest amount?

(b) Which group collected the most?

(c) Which two groups collected the same amounts?

(d) What was the total amount collected by all six form groups?

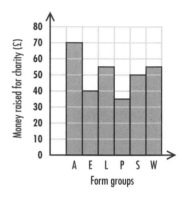

5 The bar chart shows the favourite colours chosen by a group of pupils.

(a) Which was the most popular colour?

(b) Which was the least popular colour?

(c) How many pupils chose green?

(d) What was the total number of pupils in the group?

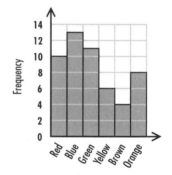

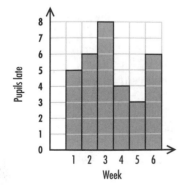

6 The bar chart shows the number of pupils in a class who were late over a six-week period.

(a) How many pupils were late in Week 6?

(b) Which week had the smallest number of pupils who were late?

(c) Which week had the largest number of pupils who were late?

(d) How many pupils were late over the six-week period?

7 The bar chart shows the total number of deliveries at a supermarket over a seven-day period.

(a) On which day was the smallest number of deliveries?

(b) On which day was the largest number of deliveries?

(c) How many deliveries were made on a Sunday?

(d) How many deliveries were made during the seven-day period?

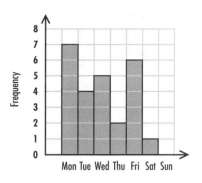

8 The bar chart shows the number of people in several age groups who chose to ride on a 'white knuckle' ride.

(a) To which age group did the largest number of people belong?

(b) To which age group did the smallest number of people belong?

(c) How many people in the 31–40 age group used the ride?

(d) How many people in the 25–30 age group used the ride?

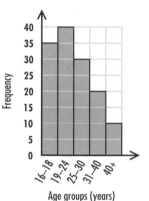

9 The bar chart shows the number of pupils taking school dinners and sandwiches on each day of a week.

(a) On which days were more pupils having sandwiches than school dinners?

(b) On which day did the smallest number of pupils have school dinners?

(c) On which day did most pupils have sandwiches?

(d) How many pupils stayed for dinners *or* sandwiches on Wednesday?

10 Pupils in six forms were asked to choose between geography and history. The bar chart shows the results of their choices.

(a) In which form was the most popular subject (i) geography (ii) history?

(b) In which form was the least popular subject (i) geography (ii) history?

(c) In which form did an equal number pick geography and history?

(d) Use the bar chart to calculate the number of pupils in each of the forms.

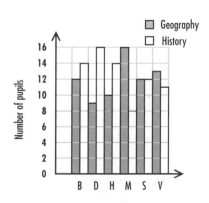

EXAMPLE

▶ Show the data given in the table as a bar chart.

Number	Tally	Frequency
0	IIII	4
1	IIII	4
2	IIII II	7
3	IIII IIII	9
4	IIII I	6
	Total	30

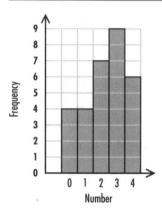

Exercise 56C

Illustrate the data in each table as a bar chart.

1

TVs	0	1	2	3	4+
Frequency	2	12	14	7	5

2

Vowels	a	e	i	o	u
Frequency	8	10	8	7	5

3

Day	Mon.	Tue.	Wed.	Thu.	Fri.
Frequency	9	8	11	10	8

4

Vehicle faults	0	1	2	3	4	5	6	7+
Frequency	4	12	9	10	8	6	4	2

5

Speed (m.p.h.)	0–10	11–20	21–30	31–40	41–50
Frequency	3	6	10	12	7

6

Pet	Frequency
Dogs	9
Cats	7
Fish	3
Mice	2
Other	5

7

Mass (kg)	Frequency
50–54	10
54–58	7
58–62	8
62–66	4

8

Length (cm)	6.0–6.9	7.0–7.9	8.0–8.9	9.0–9.9
Frequency	6	8	10	9

9

Capacity (*l*)	0–5	6–10	11–15	16–20	21–25
Frequency	11	6	8	5	3

10

Time	0900–0999	1000–1099	1100–1199	1200–1299	1300–1399	1400–1499
Frequency	3	7	5	9	6	4

Exercise 56D

Illustrate the data in each table as a bar chart.

1

Bedrooms	1	2	3	4	5+
Frequency	3	8	12	5	4

2

Children	0	1	2	3	4	5+
Frequency	5	7	12	8	4	2

3

Day	Mon.	Tue.	Wed.	Thu.	Fri.
Frequency	6	4	8	6	9

4

Marks	0–10	11–20	21–30	31–40
Frequency	2	7	12	8

5

Coins	£1	50p	10p	5p	2p	1p
Frequency	2	3	5	3	10	7

6

Fruit	Frequency
Apples	12
Bananas	5
Grapes	4
Oranges	7
Peaches	2

7

Weight (kg)	Frequency
100–149	4
150–199	7
200–249	6
250–299	9

8

Surname	A–D	E–H	I–L	M–R	S–Z
Frequency	9	7	4	5	8

9

Height (cm)	120–125	126–130	131–135	136–140	141–145
Frequency	3	8	5	4	3

10

Age range (years)	1–2	3–4	5–6	7–8	9–10
Frequency	4	6	10	8	5

57/ PICTOGRAMS

Exercise 57A

1 The pictogram shows the preferences for ice-cream flavours of a class of pupils.

Chocolate chip	
Vanilla	
Strawberry	
Mint	

(a) What was the most popular flavour?

(b) What was the least popular flavour?

(c) How many pupils chose vanilla?

(d) How many pupils are there in the class?

2 The pictogram shows the fruit taken by hospital patients.

(a) Which fruit was taken most often?

(b) Which fruit was taken least often?

(c) How many times were oranges taken?

(d) How many times were grapes taken?

Apples	
Bananas	
Oranges	
Grapes	

3 The pictogram shows the items bought by a class during break.

(a) Which item was most popular?

(b) Which two items had the same amount bought?

(c) How many crisp packets were bought?

(d) How many items were bought altogether?

Cola	
Crisps	
Chocolate bar	
Sweets	

4 The pictogram shows the type of breakfast eaten by a group of pupils.

Toast	
Cereal	
Fruit	
Cooked	
Nothing	X X X X X

(a) Which was the most popular breakfast?

(b) Which was the least popular breakfast?

(c) How many pupils had no breakfast at all?

(d) What is the total number of pupils who did have a breakfast?

5 The pictogram shows the number of houses on each of four roads.

(a) Which road has the most houses?

(b) Which road has the smallest number of houses?

(c) How many houses are there on each road?

Harbour Road	
Meadow Gate	
Frimby Street	
Howard Avenue	

= 4 houses

6 The pictogram shows the number of cars booked by a traffic warden over a four-week period.

Week 1	
Week 2	
Week 3	
Week 4	

= 10 cars

(a) How many cars were booked during each of the four weeks?

(b) What was the total number of cars booked in the four-week period?

7 The pictogram shows the number of CDs sold on a market stall over a five-day period.

Monday	⦿⦿⦿⦿⦿⦿⦿⦿
Tuesday	⦿⦿⦿⦿⦿⦿◖
Wednesday	⦿⦿⦿◖
Thursday	⦿⦿⦿⦿⦿⦿◔
Friday	⦿⦿⦿⦿⦿⦿◞

⦿ = 4 CDs

(a) How many CDs are sold on each of the five days?

(b) What is the total number of CDs sold in the five-day period?

8 The pictogram shows the number of homeworks received by each of five pupils in a week.

(a) Who has received the most homework?

(b) Who has received the least homework?

(c) Find the number of homeworks received by each of the five pupils.

Martin	▯ ▯ ▯ ▯ ▯ ▯
Gary	▯ ▯ ▯ ▯ ⌂
Maralyn	▯ ▯ ▯ ▯ ▯ ⌂
Saleem	▯ ▯ ▯ ⌂
Roger	▯ ▯ ▯ ▯ ▯

▯ = 2 homeworks

Exercise 57B

1 The pictogram shows the number of fish four friends caught in a day.

(a) Who caught the most fish?

(b) Who caught the least fish?

(c) How many fish were caught altogether?

Usman	🐟🐟🐟🐟
Helen	🐟🐟🐟🐟🐟🐟🐟
Raja	🐟🐟🐟🐟🐟
Craig	🐟🐟

2 The pictogram shows the number of milk bottles delivered to a small block of flats over a five-day period.

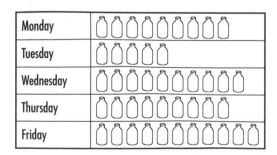

Monday	🍼🍼🍼🍼🍼🍼🍼🍼🍼
Tuesday	🍼🍼🍼🍼🍼
Wednesday	🍼🍼🍼🍼🍼🍼🍼🍼🍼🍼
Thursday	🍼🍼🍼🍼🍼🍼🍼🍼
Friday	🍼🍼🍼🍼🍼🍼🍼🍼🍼🍼🍼

(a) On which day was the most milk delivered?

(b) On which two days was the same amount of milk delivered?

(c) How many bottles of milk were delivered on Wednesday?

(d) How many bottles were delivered altogether?

3 The pictogram shows the sales on a market stall one afternoon.

(a) Which item was sold the most?

(b) Which item was sold the least?

(c) How many singles were sold?

(d) How many LPs were sold?

Singles	●●●●●●●●●
LPs	●●●●●●
CDs	●●●●●●●●●●
Tapes	▭▭▭▭▭▭

4 The pictogram shows the number of each type of drink taken in a day.

(a) Which was drunk most often?

(b) Which was drunk least?

(c) How many fruit juices were drunk?

(d) How many drinks were drunk altogether?

Tea	🍵🍵🍵🍵🍵🍵
Coffee	⬭⬭⬭⬭⬭⬭⬭⬭
Milk	🍶🍶
Fruit juice	●●●●

5 The pictogram shows how part of a family's monthly income is spent.

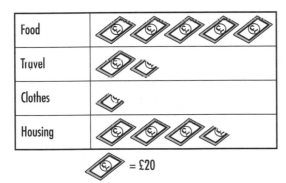

Food	💵💵💵💵💵
Travel	💵💵
Clothes	💵
Housing	💵💵💵💵

💵 = £20

(a) What is the most costly item?

(b) How much is spent on travel?

(c) How much is spent on housing?

6 The pictogram shows the number of deliveries made to a hypermarket on each day of a week.

Monday	🚚🚚🚚🚚🚚
Tuesday	🚚🚚🚚
Wednesday	🚚🚚🚚
Thursday	🚚🚚🚚🚚
Friday	🚚🚚🚚🚚

🚚 = 4 lorries

(a) On which day were the most deliveries made?

(b) On which day were the smallest number of deliveries made?

(c) How many deliveries were made on Thursday?

(d) How many deliveries were made on Wednesday?

7   The pictogram shows the number of television sets sold by an electrical discount warehouse.

(a) How many TV sets were sold in (i) Week 1 (ii) Week 2 (iii) Week 4?

(b) In which week were the smallest number of sets sold?

(c) How many TV sets were sold in Weeks 4 and 5 together?

Week 1	📺 📺 📺 📺 📺
Week 2	📺 📺 📺 📺
Week 3	📺 📺 📺 📺
Week 4	📺 📺 📺
Week 5	📺 📺 📺

📺 = 10 TVs

8   The pictogram shows the number of hours a salesman has spent travelling by various methods during a week.

Plane	🕐 🕐 🕐
Train	🕐 🕐 🕐 🕐 🕐
Car	🕐 🕐 🕐 🕐 🕐 🕐
Bus	🕐 🕐 🕐
Walk	🕐 🕐

🕐 = 4 hours

(a) How many hours were spent on a train?

(b) How many hours were spent in a car?

(c) Which form of transport was used the least?

(d) How many hours were spent travelling altogether?

Exercise 57C

Create your own symbols to draw pictograms for the following information.

1   Packets of crisps bought.

Plain	Cheese and onion	Beef	Chicken	Smoky bacon
4	8	5	4	2

2   Books needed for school.

Mon.	Tue.	Wed.	Thu.	Fri.
6	4	9	7	8

3   Hours of television seen.

BBC1	BBC2	ITV	Ch4
5	2	6	3

4   Popularity of colours.

Red	Blue	Green	Yellow	Brown
8	9	5	2	3

Create your own scaled symbols (with each symbol representing more than one unit) to draw pictograms for the following information.

5 Goals scored in a season.

Bill	Ali	Remi	Alan	Sanchez
20	10	7	9	22

6 Method of transport to school.

Walk	Bus	Car	Train	Other
28	15	18	10	7

7 Money raised for charity.

Year 7	Year 8	Year 9	Year 10	Year 11
£250	£350	£200	£150	£100

8 Young children injured on the roads.

Age range (years)	1–2	3–4	5–6	7–8	9–10
Number of children	9	16	24	20	18

Exercise 57D

Create your own symbols to draw pictograms for the following information.

1 Hours of sunshine per day.

Mon.	Tue.	Wed.	Thu.	Fri.
8	7	6	5	8

2 Hours spent on each activity per day.

Sleep	Work	Eating	Travel	Other
8	7	2	2	5

3 Choices of reading material.

Crime	Mystery	Sci-fi	Romance	Adventure
5	6	9	4	7

4 Holiday destinations.

UK	France	Spain	USA	Other
8	5	11	2	9

Create your own scaled symbols (with each symbol representing more than one unit) to draw pictograms for the following information.

5 Pupils with birthdays on each day.

Mon.	Tue.	Wed.	Thu.	Fri.	Sat.	Sun.
20	28	20	14	25	18	17

6 Cars using a car-park at particular times.

10 a.m.	11 a.m.	12 noon	1 p.m.	2 p.m.	3 p.m.	4 p.m.
200	230	300	400	350	350	300

7 Preferred types of music.

Soul	Dance	Rock	Country	Heavy metal
24	18	16	12	10

8 Preferred drinks.

Milk	Coffee	Tea	Cola	Fruit juice
8	20	15	28	12

REVISION

Exercise F

1 Draw a frequency table to summarise this data.

```
6   4   8   9   5   7   7   8   8   4   6   9   5   9
8   7   5   8   6   6   9   4   7   4   9   7   8   6
7   6   4   9   7   7   6   8   6   7   5   4
```

2 Draw a frequency table to summarise this data.

```
A   E   F   B   E   A   D   C   F   B   F   E   E   D
E   F   D   A   C   E   E   B   A   A   D   B   F   E
F   A   F   E   B   D   C   F   E   C   A   B
```

3 Draw a bar chart to represent the information in the table, which shows the number of buses arriving late at a depot.

Day	Monday	Tuesday	Wednesday	Thursday	Friday
Frequency	8	7	9	10	6

4 Draw a bar chart to represent the information in the table, which shows the number of each length of wood in a yard.

Length	1 m	2 m	3 m	4 m	5 m
Frequency	9	14	12	7	5

5 Draw a pictogram to represent the information in the table, which shows the number of goals scored by each of several players in a season.

Player	Alan	Ali	Adam	Anthony	Adama
Frequency	4	10	8	6	7

6 Draw a pictogram to represent the information in the table, which shows the number of people in a Pizza Parlour at various times during the day.

Time	10 a.m.	11 a.m.	12 noon	1 p.m.	2 p.m.	3 p.m.	4 p.m.	5 p.m.
Frequency	8	15	24	21	19	16	13	18

Exercise FF

1 This is a train timetable.

Shrewsbury	—	—	—	—	0556	—	—	0615	0640	0715
Telford Central	—	—	—	—	0615	—	—	0636	0702	0735
Wolverhampton	0519	0549	0619	—	0649	—	—	0719	0749	0819
Sandwell & Dudley	0529	0559	0629	—	0659	—	—	0729	0759	0829
Birmingham New St	0545	0615	0645	—	0715	0733	—	0745	0815	0845
Birmingham Intern'l ⊕	0556	0626	0656	—	0726	0744	—	0756	0826	0856
Coventry	0607	0637	0707	—	0737	—	—	0807	0837	0907
Rugby	0619	0649	0719	0730	0751	—	0805	—	0851	—
Milton Keynes Central	0644	—	0825	—	—	—	—	0840	—	0939
Watford Junction	0742	—	0857	—	—	—	—	—	0941s	—
London Euston	0733	0758	0828	0840	0902	0906	0911	0928	1004	1027

(a) At what time does the 0745 train from Birmingham New St arrive at London Euston?

(b) At what time does the 0619 train from Wolverhampton arrive at Rugby?

(c) How long does it take the 0529 train from Sandwell to get to Milton Keynes?

(d) How long does it take the 0819 train from Wolverhampton to get to London Euston?

(e) Shazia lives in Sandwell, and needs to be in Coventry by 0700. What is the time of the latest train she could catch?

(f) Bill wants to catch a train from Birmingham New St to London Euston to arrive no later than 0915. What is the time of the latest train he could catch?

2 The bar chart shows the number of babies born in a hospital in a week.

(a) On which day was the greatest number of babies born?

(b) On which day was the smallest number of babies born?

(c) On which two days were the same number of babies born?

(d) How many fewer babies were born on Tuesday than on Monday?

(e) How many babies were born altogether over the seven-day period?

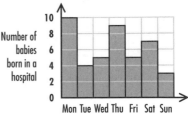

3 The pictogram shows the numbers of various types of plant.

(a) Of which plant is there the most?

(b) Of which plant is there the least?

(c) How many lupins are there?

(d) How many bushes are there?

(e) How many plants are there altogether?

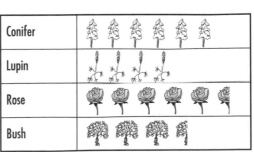

= 2 plants

58/ INTERPRETING DIAGRAMS

Exercise 58A

1   The graph shows the number of times each score on a dice was thrown.

   (a) How many times was '1' thrown?

   (b) Which score was thrown the most?

   (c) Which score was thrown the least?

   (d) Which two scores were thrown the same number of times?

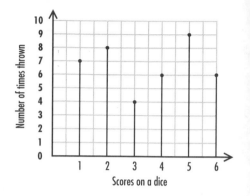

2   The depth of water in an estuary is read each hour.

   (a) What is the depth of water at 1100 hours?

   (b) What is the depth of water at 1500 hours?

   (c) At what time is the depth $9\frac{1}{2}$ metres?

   (d) Between which two times does the depth remain the same?

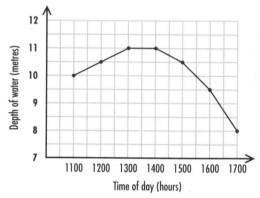

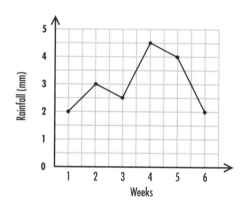

3   The graph shows the amount of rainfall recorded each week over a period of six weeks.

   (a) What was the highest record of rainfall?

   (b) During which week was a rainfall of 4 mm recorded?

   (c) What was the rainfall during Week 2?

4   The graph is a record of a hospital patient's temperature.

   (a) When was the temperature at a maximum?

   (b) What was the maximum temperature?

   (c) What was the temperature at 1000 hours on Tuesday?

   (d) What was the temperature at 1800 hours on Monday?

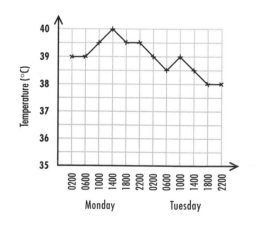

5 The graph is a record of the months of the year in which the birthdays of a group of people fall.

(a) In which month were the most people born?

(b) In which month was the smallest number of people born?

(c) How many people were born in (i) February (ii) August?

(d) In which months were exactly five people born?

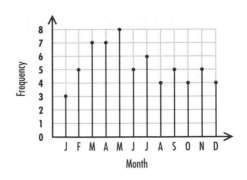

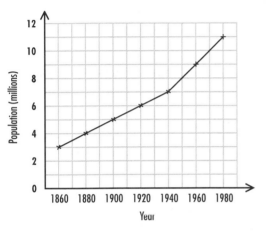

6 The graph shows the population of a country, rounded to the nearest million people.

(a) In which year was the population seven million?

(b) What was the population in (i) 1880 (ii) 1980?

(c) What was the population increase between (i) 1920 and 1940 (ii) 1940 and 1960?

7 The graph shows the number of cars in a city-centre car-park at various times in the day.

(a) What is the maximum number of cars in the car-park?

(b) At what time are there the most cars in the car-park?

(c) How many cars were there in the car-park at (i) noon (ii) 10 p.m.?

(d) At what time was the number of cars (i) 20 (ii) 16?

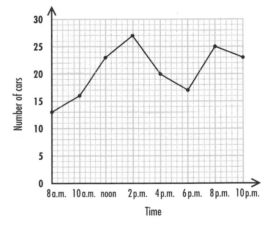

8 The graph shows the temperature of water in a container as it cools.

(a) What was the temperature after (i) 2 min (ii) 8 min (iii) 5 min?

(b) How many minutes had gone by when the temperature was (i) 42°C (ii) 45°C (iii) 41.2°C?

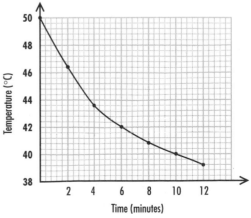

1 The graph shows a golfer's score at each of eighteen holes.

(a) What was her score at hole number (i) 5 (ii) 9 (iii) 15?

(b) At which holes did she score (i) 4 (ii) 5?

(c) Which were her five best holes?

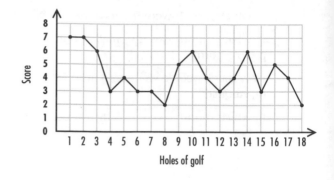

Holes of golf

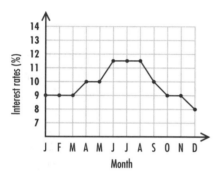

Month

2 The graph shows the interest rates over a 12-month period.

(a) What was the interest rate in (i) February (ii) September?

(b) During which months was the interest rate 10%?

(c) Between which two months was the sharpest fall in interest rates?

3 Cards were drawn from a pack and their suit noted. The graph shows how many of each suit were drawn.

(a) Which suit was drawn most often?

(b) Which suit was drawn least often?

(c) How many times was a card drawn from the pack?

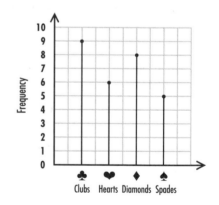

4 The graph shows a record of the number of jackets sold in a clothes shop.

(a) How many jackets were sold during (i) Week 3 (ii) Week 8?

(b) During which weeks were (i) 17 (ii) 16 jackets sold?

(c) How many jackets were sold during the first five weeks?

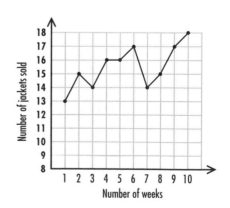

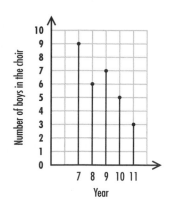

5 The graph shows the number of boys from each year group who are in the choir.

(a) How many boys are in the choir from (i) Year 7 (ii) Year 10?

(b) Which year group has the fewest number of boys in the choir?

(c) How many boys are in the choir altogether?

6 The graph shows the number of shirts made at a factory during a particular week.

(a) On which day were the most shirts made?

(b) On which day was the smallest number of shirts made?

(c) How many shirts were made on each of the days?

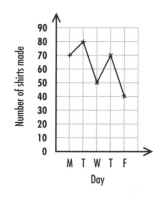

7 The graph shows the cost of buying a holiday during a particular week of the year.

(a) What is the cheapest week to go on the holiday?

(b) What are the dearest weeks to go on the holiday?

(c) What is the cost in the (i) 1st week of June (ii) 3rd week of August?

(d) At what time is the cost (i) £520 (ii) £580?

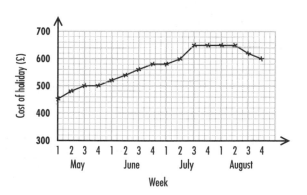

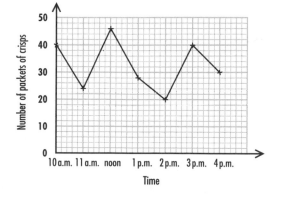

8 The graph shows the number of packets of crisps in a school snack machine.

(a) How many crisps are there in the machine at (i) 1 p.m. (ii) 3 p.m.?

(b) At what times does the snack machine have (i) 40 packets (ii) 20 packets?

(c) The machine is filled twice. Between which two pairs of times is the machine filled?

59/ DRAWING BAR LINE GRAPHS

EXAMPLE

▶ Show the data in the table as a bar line graph.

Score on dice	1	2	3	4	5	6
Frequency	8	6	5	7	6	7

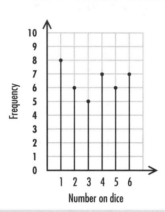

Exercise 59A

Draw bar line graphs for each of the following tables.

1

Score on dice	1	2	3	4	5	6
Frequency	6	9	8	7	8	5

2

Vowels	a	e	i	o	u
Frequency	8	9	7	7	6

3

Pets	Dogs	Cats	Fish	Rabbits	Mice
Frequency	7	9	4	2	2

4

Day	Mon.	Tue.	Wed.	Thu.	Fri.
Lates	8	6	5	7	9

5

Shape	Square	Triangle	Circle	Diamond	Rectangle
Frequency	14	16	9	12	7

6	Pupil	Ali	Bill	Carol	Diane	Errol
	Score	18	23	15	21	16

7	Day	Mon.	Tue.	Wed.	Thu.	Fri.	Sat.
	Takings (£)	80	90	60	90	110	130

8	Month	J	F	M	A	M	J	J	A	S	O	N	D
	Late trains	9	12	10	7	6	8	5	4	7	8	10	9

Exercise 59B

Draw bar line graphs for each of the following tables.

1	Suit	Hearts	Diamonds	Clubs	Spades
	Frequency	8	9	8	6

2	Number of pets	0	1	2	3	4	5
	Frequency	8	11	6	4	2	3

3	Score on dice	1	2	3	4	5	6
	Frequency	8	7	10	9	8	7

4	Day	Mon.	Tue.	Wed.	Thu.	Fri.
	Fish caught	6	10	0	8	7

5	Year	1992	1993	1994	1995	1996
	Intake	180	182	178	180	184

6	Week	1	2	3	4	5	6
	Test mark (%)	70	60	65	80	75	80

7	Pupil	Joan	Keith	Chris	Dee	Sybil	Gwyn
	Pints of milk (per week)	8	7	12	10	4	9

8	Week	1	2	3	4	5	6	7	8
	Gallons of petrol	8	9	0	5	6	0	7	7

60/ DRAWING LINE GRAPHS

EXAMPLE

▶ Show the data in the table as a line graph.

Day	Mon.	Tue.	Wed.	Thu.	Fri.
Absences	5	4	4	6	7

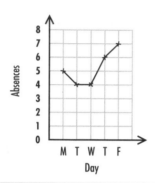

Exercise 60A

Draw line graphs for each of the following tables.

1

Day	Mon.	Tue.	Wed.	Thu.	Fri.
Mugs painted	22	31	33	35	25

2

Time	10 a.m.	11 a.m.	noon	1 p.m.	2 p.m.	3 p.m.	4 p.m.
People queuing	12	8	7	15	13	9	10

3 The number of deaths in a village from the 1678 plague.

Month	Jan.	Feb.	Mar.	Apr.	May	Jun.	Jul.	Aug.
Deaths	3	4	10	18	16	11	5	3

4

Day	Sun.	Mon.	Tue.	Wed.	Thu.	Fri.	Sat.
Airplane departures	35	24	26	23	29	36	42

5 Fuel consumption figures at various speeds.

Average speed (km/h)	30	40	50	60	70	80	90	100	110	120
Litres per 100 km	13	12	9	7.5	6.5	5	5	6	7	9

6

Month	Mar.	Apr.	May	Jun.	Jul.	Aug.	Sep.	Oct.
People rescued	2	6	12	8	14	10	8	2

7

Meal	Breakfast	Lunch	Tea	Breakfast	Lunch	Tea
Calories	440	630	920	410	640	830

8

Week	1	2	3	4	5	6	7	8
Gallons of petrol	8	9	0	5	6	0	7	7

Exercise 60B

Draw line graphs for each of the following tables.

1

Day	Mon.	Tue.	Wed.	Thu.	Fri.	Sat.
Dinner sets packed	42	39	40	41	29	25

2

Miles per gallon	10	20	30	40	50	60
Litres per 100 km	20	15	9	7	5	4

3

Day	Sun.	Mon.	Tue.	Wed.	Thu.	Fri.	Sat.
Call-outs	8	4	5	3	5	6	7

4

Month	Apr.	May	Jun.	Jul.	Aug.	Sep.	Oct.	Nov.	Dec.
Deaths	8	10	12	22	24	22	13	7	3

5

Week	1	2	3	4	5	6
Knife attacks	20	21	9	7	4	6

6

Week	1	2	3	4	5	6	7	8
Subscriptions paid	18	14	15	21	24	16	19	15

7

Month	Jan.	Feb.	Mar.	Apr.	May.	Jun.	Jul.	Aug.	Sep.
Assaults	5	6	6	10	11	20	45	28	13

8

Year	1986	1987	1988	1989	1990	1991	1992	1993
Car sales	70	72	90	94	89	83	85	89

61/ GROUPING DATA

There are some occasions when it is useful to group data together.

> **EXAMPLE**
>
> ▶ Group this data together in a frequency table.
>
> | 76 | 69 | 65 | 63 | 70 | 90 | 75 | 22 | 88 | 49 | 38 |
> |----|----|----|----|----|----|----|----|----|----|----|
> | 92 | 72 | 39 | 67 | 27 | 47 | 68 | 78 | 72 | 74 | 19 |
> | 85 | 48 | 52 | 93 | 49 | 83 | 58 | 50 |
>
> The groups 0–9, 10–19, etc. are called **class intervals**.
>
> | Mark | Tally | Frequency |
> |------|-------|-----------|
> | 0–9 | | 0 |
> | 10–19 | I | 1 |
> | 20–29 | II | 2 |
> | 30–39 | II | 2 |
> | 40–49 | IIII | 4 |
> | 50–59 | III | 3 |
> | 60–69 | ЖЖ | 5 |
> | 70–79 | ЖЖ II | 7 |
> | 80–89 | III | 3 |
> | 90–99 | III | 3 |
> | | TOTAL | 30 |

Exercise 61A

For each set of data draw and complete a frequency table.

1
12	18	16	13	10	7	8	12	8	11	15	14	16	1	3
15	18	14	11	18	5	7	9	16	18	7	8	9	14	2
4	15	18	8	3

Use class intervals 0–4, 5–9, etc.

2
80	82	68	79	84	48	63	45	59	71	65	88	87	76	31
33	64	46	63	66	62	72	73	78	81	58	51	54	83	33
68	61	72	78	83	80	43	80	48	34

Use class intervals 30–39, 40–49, etc.

3
28	28	27	17	17	18	24	28	18	19	28	22	26	17	21
25	12	23	18	19	20	28	16	28	21	27	18	22	26	20
25	23	28	13	24	25	19	18	11	14

Use class intervals 10–14, 15–19, etc.

4

87	61	49	38	69	63	63	61	67	53	40	35	74	68	27
54	65	48	58	40	38	86	61	56	42	58	55	50	36	28
61	80	41	50	57	46	27	44	72	50	45	44	52	72	28

Use class intervals 20–29, 30–39, etc.

5 Weights given on packets of food.

430 g	340 g	414 g	340 g	175 g	215 g	225 g	400 g	439 g	300 g	120 g	225 g
305 g	300 g	325 g	425 g	300 g	235 g	280 g	218 g	180 g	170 g	300 g	340 g
325 g	225 g	243 g	275 g	300 g	280 g	360 g	380 g	283 g	380 g	343 g	

Use class intervals 100 g–149 g, 150 g–199 g, etc.

6 Amounts spent in a shop.

£16.76	£28.54	£8.93	£26.22	£41.50	£33.57	£29.46	£12.72	£31.80	£40.52
£38.88	£26.63	£12.99	£18.49	£38.63	£12.73	£31.74	£21.24	£14.80	£20.66
£27.04	£16.29	£10.65	£16.88	£15.81					

Use class intervals £0.00–£9.99, £10.00–£19.99, etc.

7 Ages of people in a survey. Use your own class intervals.

28	26	38	29	27	27	39	17	38	29	42	42	45	28	40
47	33	17	28	27	36	46	38	36	63	63	35	40	51	63
55	24	39	45	40	21	38	49	29	51					

8 Percentage test marks. Use your own class intervals.

69%	32%	91%	83%	46%	36%	53%	80%	71%	82%	50%	57%
30%	34%	66%	89%	49%	71%	87%	68%	41%	93%	70%	70%
66%	92%	94%	86%	58%	82%	38%	68%	83%	94%	92%	45%
46%	84%	68%	67%	51%	81%	33%	28%	78%	29%	58%	46%
37%	71%										

9 Points awarded in a competition.

52.4	59.7	58.4	58.4	56.2	63.1	57.1	56.6	62.1	60.3	57.0	61.3
55.1	63.5	61.8	64.5	56.2	61.3	54.8	65.2	60.1	55.9	55.3	58.2
53.4	51.9	57.8	54.8	51.4	57.7						

Use class intervals 50.0–53.9, 54.0–57.9, etc.

10 Mileage travelled in a day. Use your own class intervals.

27.7	45.8	38.8	43.9	50.9	37.8	52.2	55.8	37.6	35.4	53.3	71.4
41.3	31.8	23.6	12.5	47.2	20.9	26.6	39.2	41.8	13.6	17.4	65.3
61.7	74.2	41.7	26.7	78.4	54.4	36.2	47.8	39.4	54.2	61.4	

Exercise 61B

1

68	40	57	46	74	32	85	56	70	81	71	81	38	29	75
83	83	38	52	48	67	75	80	67	64	37	28	45	84	68
88	79	61	82	57										

Use class intervals of 10–19, 20–29, etc.

2

32	25	20	28	10	14	18	18	11	9	12	23	20	25	32
19	34	18	26	39	15	30	14	5	30	3	6	4	8	26
2	12	37	23	30	7									

Use class intervals of 0–4, 5–9, etc.

3

23	38	29	17	27	39	37	18	39	42	42	25	28	30	47
33	38	37	36	46	38	26	23	63	35	40	41	63	45	24
19	45	40	31	18	26	29	19	27	11					

Use class intervals of 10–19, 20–29, etc.

4

24	26	24	26	27	26	22	22	23	23	24	23	21	14	19
13	20	28	23	17	22	28	23	26	25	28	26	27	21	17
23	12	24	19	18	27	26	28	14	18					

Use class intervals of 10–14, 15–19, etc.

5

£26	£21	£12	£5	£12	£31	£30	£9	£28	£17	£12	£20
£17	£3	£23	£8	£17	£8	£13	£3	£11	£22	£28	£32
£15	£24	£23	£2	£7	£27	£18	£25	£30	£12	£19	£13
£16	£19	£16	£32								

Use class intervals of £0–£4, £5–£9, etc.

6 Videos hired each day from a video rental shop.

54	63	10	32	51	64	58	48	8	30	58	52	63	43	28
55	24	7	50	48	68	37	68	31	46	67	12	47	32	20
63	58	49	40	32	58	24	32	47	20	55	18	53	38	14
19	14	60	54	49										

Use class intervals of 0–9, 10–19, etc.

7 Percentage test marks. Use your own class intervals.

60	74	80	88	71	83	86	81	60	48	66	62	44	85	66
46	64	76	80	71	50	84	64	85	88	80	54	52	69	89
67	79	51	80	71	89	67	39	36	46	83	41	32	59	57
60	72	71	70	43										

8 Amounts spent on a day trip. Use your own class intervals.

£5.74	£44.77	£28.01	£37.38	£18.62	£8.31	£22.77	£45.62	£38.01	£10.42
£25.81	£29.05	£16.33	£6.46	£19.20	£18.80	£30.68	£27.05	£26.28	£10.94
£21.24	£31.28	£46.73	£28.26	£49.18	£29.13	£36.63	£18.88	£30.52	£45.45

9 A record of the weights of pre-packed meats.

1.86 g	1.58 g	0.97 g	1.92 g	0.98 g	1.97 g	0.73 g	2.93 g	1.62 g	0.87 g	2.09 g	1.93 g
0.46 g	1.04 g	1.42 g	2.12 g	1.08 g	2.76 g	1.27 g	2.45 g	0.16 g	0.87 g	0.44 g	2.51 g
1.72 g	0.94 g	2.31 g	2.44 g	1.21 g	2.12 g						

Use class intervals of 0.00 g–0.49 g, 0.50 g–0.99 g, etc.

10 Speeds of passing cars on a road. Use your own class intervals.

37.4	31.1	22.3	15.9	38.8	26.6	48.6	9.5	30.3	27.2	35.4	31.7
42.8	36.3	29.4	7.2	23.5	31.2	39.8	47.0	32.1	38.4	30.3	20.8
35.0	38.1	8.7	27.4	23.6	12.5	37.8	41.7	41.2	26.7	17.4	

62/ MODE AND MEDIAN

Two averages that are easily found are the mode and the median.
The **mode** is the one of which there is the most.
The **median** is the one which is strictly in the middle of the ordered list.

> **EXAMPLE**
>
> ▶ 5   2   9   6   3   10   4   6   2   8   9   7   3
>   5   12   8   2   11   10   6   9   7   6   12   7
>
> Find (a) the mode and (b) the median of the list of numbers.
>
> First write the list in numerical order:
> 2 2 2 3 3 4 5 5 6 6 6 6 7 7 7 8 8 9 9 9 10 10 11 12 12
>   ↑ middle number
> (a) The mode is the number 6, since there are more 6s than any other number.
> (b) The median is the number 7.
>   There are 25 numbers. The middle number is the 13th one in the list.
>
> When there is no strict middle value, the median is the number in between the middle two numbers.
>
> 2 2 3 3 4 4 5 5 6 6 7 7
>   ↑ the middle value is 4.5 or $4\frac{1}{2}$

Exercise 62A

For each set of numbers find (a) the mode (b) the median.

1   2, 2, 3, 3, 3, 4, 5, 5, 5, 5, 6, 6, 7   **2**   0, 1, 1, 1, 1, 2, 2, 3, 3, 3, 4, 4, 5, 5, 5

3   4, 4, 5, 5, 5, 6, 7, 7, 7, 8, 9, 9, 10, 10, 10, 10

4   2, 2, 3, 3, 3, 4, 5, 5, 6, 7, 7, 7, 7, 8, 8, 9

5   4, 4, 6, 9, 8, 3, 5, 4, 6   **6**   8, 5, 6, 6, 4, 7, 7, 4, 7, 5, 6, 7

7   55, 60, 53, 51, 52, 40, 51, 52, 51   **8**   13, 20, 15, 13, 16, 15, 12, 13, 18

9   8, 8, 5, 8, 4, 6, 8, 5, 6   **10**   7, 11, 11, 8, 7, 8, 11, 15, 14

11   8, 14, 27, 39, 28, 12, 35, 29, 19, 23, 18, 6, 12

12   9, 15, 10, 15, 12, 9, 8, 6, 3, 8, 8, 5

13

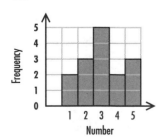

14

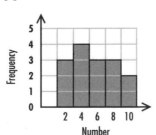

15

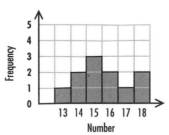

Exercise 62B

For each set of numbers find (a) the mode (b) the median.

1   4, 4, 5, 5, 5, 6, 7, 7, 8, 8, 8, 8, 9, 9, 10

2   9, 9, 10, 10, 11, 11, 11, 12, 12, 13, 13, 14, 14

3   4, 5, 6, 6, 6, 7, 7, 8, 8, 9, 9, 9, 9, 10, 10, 11

4   0, 0, 1, 1, 1, 2, 2, 3, 3, 3, 4, 4, 4, 4, 5, 5, 5, 6, 6, 7

5   4, 4, 3, 6, 5, 1, 1, 2, 5, 2, 2, 1, 5, 1, 6

6   27, 24, 24, 29, 32, 35, 29, 24,

7   35, 34, 34, 31, 32, 36, 34, 30, 32, 33, 35

8   25, 27, 13, 18, 10, 23, 23, 12, 29, 20, 15, 21, 13, 23, 27

9   10, 4, 7, 3, 8, 11, 9, 8, 9, 10, 9

10   15, 15, 16, 13, 11, 13, 14, 12, 13, 12, 16, 14, 14, 15, 13

11   10, 12, 8, 20, 12, 15, 14, 12, 12, 16, 23

12   15, 16, 16, 7, 6, 10, 17, 14, 15, 8, 20, 10, 15, 18, 3, 12, 16, 17, 12, 19, 9, 16

13   **14**   **15**

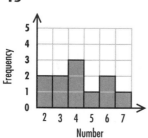
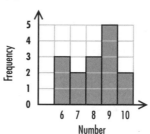
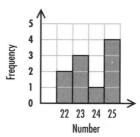

63/ PROBABILITY SCALE

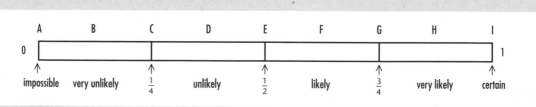

This is a probability scale.

The **probability** of an event happening can be shown as a position on the scale.

'Evens ' is a term which is used to describe events which are equally likely to happen. This is normally indicated by the midpoint position in the table.

► Events which will never happen (impossible) are shown at position A.

Events which will certainly happen are shown at position I.

Events which have a 1 in 4 chance of happening are shown at position C.

Events which are unlikely, but have more than a 1 in 4 chance of happening are shown at position D.

The probability of a student receiving homework on a particular night is 'likely', and can be shown at position F on the probability scale.

Exercise 63A

For each statement below write down the letter of the position on the probability scale at which it could be shown.

1 Paris is the capital of France.

2 I throw a coin and get a 'tail'.

3 It will snow tomorrow.

4 I pick a diamond card from a pack of cards.

5 Next year will have 12 months.

6 A person will run a distance of 100 metres without stopping.

7 I throw a '5' with a dice.

8 A watch stops between 3, 4, 5, or 6.

9 A new-born baby is a girl.

10 The moon is made of yellow cheese.

11 Picking a red pen at random from a box containing five red and three blue pens.

12 6×4 is the same as 12×2.

13 I pick a Queen from a pack of cards.

14 I will need to spend some money today.

15 At least one train is late arriving at a station during the day.

16 Throwing an even number on a dice.

17 Winning a raffle at school.

18 I throw a '9' with a dice.

19 A clock stops between 12, 1, 2, ..., 8 or 9.

20 I get the number 1 or 2 when throwing a dice.

Exercise 63B

For each statement below write down the letter of the position on the probability scale at which it could be shown.

1 It will get dark tonight.

2 A new-born baby is a boy.

3 I will score 100% in my next maths test.

4   A clock stops between 6, 7, 8, or 9.

5   A blue pen is picked at random from a box containing three blue pens and one black pen.

6   Next year will have 13 months.

7   An adult picked at random will have watched more ITV programmes than those on any other channel.

8   I pick a heart from a pack of cards.

9   A bus will break down on the way to school.

10   The weather will change during a particular week.

11   We will have rain in the next 12 months.

12   I get a 5 or 6 when throwing a dice,

13   I will be late home from school at least once this term.

14   A tossed coin will land on its edge.

15   A year selected at random will not be a leap year.

16   February 30th is on a Sunday next year.

17   Throwing an odd number on a dice.

18   We will have frost on at least one day this year.

19   The sun will rise tomorrow.

20   A light switch will be switched ON.

64/ OUTCOMES

When an event happens, the **outcomes** are what might happen.

EXAMPLE

▶

Two coins are thrown together. All the possible solutions are:

Head Head   Head Tail   Tail Head   Tail Tail

Exercise 64A

For each situation write out a list of all the possible outcomes.

1   Throwing a single dice.

2   Picking a letter from the first five letters of the alphabet.

3   Throwing a dart at a dart board.

4   Picking a number from a clock face.

5   Throwing three coins together.

6 Throwing the spinner.

7 Throwing a dice and a coin together.

8 Throwing these spinners together.

9 Throwing these spinners together.

10 Throwing two dice together.

11 Choosing two different days in the week, for example Mon./Tue.

12 Picking three beads from a bag containing 20 yellow, 20 black and 20 white beads.

Exercise 64B

For each situation write out a list of all the possible outcomes.

1 Throwing a single coin.

2 Picking a number from the first eight numbers (1–8).

3 Picking a vowel from the letters of the alphabet.

4 Picking any day from the seven days of·the week.

5 Picking an even number from all the numbers less than 15.

6 Picking any letter from the word ABRACADABRA

7 Throwing two octagonal dice together.

8 Throwing these spinners together.

9 Throwing these spinners together.

10 Picking three beads from a bag containing 20 blue and 20 red beads.

11 Picking three beads from a bag containing 20 blue, 20 red and 20 green beads.

12 Throwing four coins together.

REVISION

Exercise G

1 Draw a bar line graph for this table.

Score	4	5	6	7	8	9
Frequency	3	5	8	7	7	4

2 Draw a line graph for this table.

Day	Sun.	Mon.	Tue.	Wed.	Thu.	Fri.	Sat.
Bottles	7	5	8	7	6	6	7

3 Draw a bar line graph for this table.

Letter	A	B	C	D	E	F	G	H
Frequency	4	6	6	5	10	3	4	6

4 Draw a line graph for this table.

Month	Jan.	Feb.	Mar.	Apr.	May.	Jun.
Babies born	4	3	6	7	6	5

5 (a) For the set of data below draw and complete a frequency table.
Use class intervals 0–9, 10–19, etc.

```
10   6   30   41   13   52   33    4   45   21   57   14   28   17
44  37   18   52    3   56   13   44   26   47    9   58   38   46
61  55   22   66   49   39   66   24   69
```

(b) Draw a bar chart for your table.

6 (a) For this set of data draw and complete a frequency table. Use class intervals of 0–4, 5–9, etc.

```
25    6   28    1   26   10   15   17    3   18    9   21   12   24
28   31   16   12   33   19   26   13   32   22    7   16   22   27
24    9   17   32   14
```

(a) Draw a bar chart for your table.

7 For each of the following set of numbers find (i) the mode (ii) the median.
(a) 2, 2, 3, 3, 3, 4, 4, 4, 5, 5, 5, 5, 5
(b) 1, 1, 1, 2, 2, 3, 3, 4, 4, 4, 4, 4, 5, 5
(c) 20, 22, 14, 15, 25, 22, 17, 13, 22, 14, 24
(d) 45, 50, 46, 40, 46, 42, 54, 46, 43, 45, 53, 48, 44, 42

Exercise GG

1 The bar line graph shows the number of points gained by five competitors.

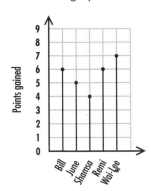

(a) Who gained the most points?

(b) Which two competitors gained the same number of points?

(c) How many points were awarded to Jane?

2 The graph shows the number of students seen by a home tutor each day.

(a) On which day were the most students seen?

(b) On which day were six students seen?

(c) How many students were seen on Monday?

(d) How many students were seen altogether?

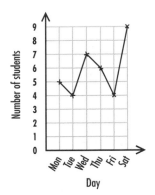

3 The graph shows a series of temperature recordings over 4-hourly intervals.

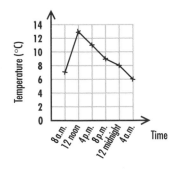

(a) At which recorded time was the temperature the highest?

(b) What was the highest recorded temperature?

(c) Between which two recorded times was the temperature fall the least?

4 In a game the following throws of a dice were recorded:
1, 4, 2, 5, 6, 3, 6, 6, 4, 4, 1, 5, 3, 4, 1, 2, 5, 3, 4, 5, 1, 4, 5, 2, 2, 6, 5, 4, 2, 6, 3

(a) Draw and complete a frequency table to summarise this data.

(b) Draw a bar line graph for your table.

(c) What is the modal value (that is, which number occurs the most)?

5 The following amounts of money were collected as sponsor money.

£18.35	£35,03	£7.85	£31.07	£47.38	£16.38	£53.25	£25.36	£23.40	£66.10
£16.54	£19.58	£26.40	£33.52	£6.27	£33.20	£39.48	£9.15	£43.02	£61.54
£13.00	£71.55	£17.35	£73.41	£15.53	£41.22	£27.14	£5.13	£38.47	£35.27
£44.43	£57.55	£26.58	£12.28	£35.30	£29.05	£62.12	£11.15	£49.48	£20.22

(a) Draw and complete a frequency table to summarise this data. Use your own class intervals.

(b) Draw a bar chart for your data.

(c) What is the modal class interval (that is, which class interval has the greatest frequency)?

6 A letter is picked at random from the last ten letters of the alphabet. Write down a list of all the possible letters which could be picked.

7 Two coins and a dice are thrown together. Write down a list of all the possible outcomes.

8

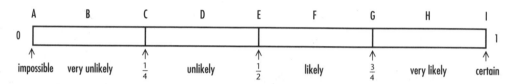

For each statement below write down the letter of the position on the probability scale at which it should be shown.

(a) A jumbo jet will make a safe landing on the playground.

(b) A coin is tossed and lands showing 'heads'.

(c) During a particular month a steam train carried on the back of a lorry will drive along a motorway.

(d) The earth will travel once around the sun during this year.

(e) During a particular week at least one person in the class will have their hair cut.